The Temper of Western Europe

GARDNER WEBB COLLEGE LIBRARY

Crane Brinton

The Temper
of Western Europe

GREENWOOD PRESS, PUBLISHERS
WESTPORT, CONNECTICUT

GARDNER WEBB COLLEGE LIBRARY

Copyright © 1953 by the President and Fellows of Harvard College

Reprinted by permission
of Harvard University Press

First Greenwood Reprinting 1970

SBN 8371-2799-8

PRINTED IN UNITED STATES OF AMERICA

D
1051
.B75
1970

To my friends in

Charlottesville

Prefatory Note

This book is an expansion of the James W. Richard Lectures in History delivered at the University of Virginia on April 21, 22, and 23, 1953. I wish to thank the authorities at the University for giving me this early opportunity, after my return from Europe, to organize my impressions of the temper of Western Europeans. I must thank also Mr. Thomas J. Wilson, Director of the Harvard University Press, and his staff for their collaboration in the task of bringing out this book with a speed imposed by the subject but taxing severely the sound traditions of university publishing. I thank once more my secretary, Miss Elizabeth F. Hoxie, for her care in the preparation of the manuscript.

Crane Brinton

Peacham, Vermont
August 20, 1953

Contents

Western Europe: Dying or Living?

"The period through which we are living presents itself as one of unmitigated confusion and disintegration . . . "

"We can assert with some confidence that our own period is one of decline; that the standards of culture are lower than they were fifty years ago; and that the evidences of this decline are visible in every department of human activity."

"For myself, and I was not alone, all the conscious and recollected years of my life have been lived to this day under the heavy threat of world catastrophe, and most of the energies of my mind and spirit have been spent in the effort to grasp the meaning of these threats, to trace them to their sources and to understand the logic of this majestic and terrible failure of the life of man in the Western World."

To these wails from Lewis Mumford, T. S. Eliot, and Katherine Anne Porter, which Mr. William Shirer uses as an epigraph for his own wake over the corpse of Europe, *Midcentury Journey*, one may add dozens from Mr. Shirer's book alone. The star of France is waning; in Germany the Master Race is at it again; there will probably not always be an England. Mr. Shirer's plane did but touch down at the great—and lively—Shannon airport. The plane stayed long enough, however, to allow Mr. Shirer to confirm his natural feeling that something was wrong in Ireland. "Now that its great political struggle against Britain had been won there was every reason to believe that a free and independent Ireland would flower as never before.

"But somehow, even after a new constitution, hammered out by De Valera in 1937, proclaimed Ireland to be a sovereign, independent, democratic state, cutting off almost the last slender ties with the British Commonwealth and king and re-establishing the old Gaelic name of Eire, and even after the last threads of connection were severed and Eire became, on Easter Monday, April 18, 1949, 'the Republic of Ireland,' the dream faded, the great objectives were lost sight of and Ireland struck even such a sympathetic observer as this one as a community whose vision had narrowed, a parochial place preoccupied with pettiness, content to remove itself from the major currents of Western life and thought, intent on censoring good books and denying many of its greatest writers. Freedom, by some queer quirk of reversal, appeared to have dulled the fine creativeness of a poetic and imaginative people."

Mr. Arthur Koestler is an even gloomier witness. His *Age of Longing* is a novel of postwar Western Europe, with the scene for the most part in Paris and with a thoroughly modern international cast of weak, unhappy, and frustrated characters, interspersed with a few stronger but even more depraved ones. There is a Communist of course who knows where he is going—and it is a most unpleasant place. We need not concern ourselves with the details of the story. One character, however, symbolizes nicely Mr. Koestler's feeling of hopelessness. This is an aged French aristocrat, a bundle of nastiness. He is full of obsessions which, since his creator is Mr. Koestler, spill over into symbols of our present distress. He has a special obsession about the prostate gland, and the France, indeed the whole West, of his time comes out as a swollen prostate. This is indeed a neat figure of speech. In one unpleasant symbol Mr. Koestler combines the worst he can feel about our times: old age and impotence and disease. No therapy, not even surgery, will save this French aristocrat and the world he symbolizes.

As a final exhibit I should like to add an excerpt from a private letter from a most sensitive and distinguished literary friend of mine, an American in Paris: "Paris, even in its old age is exciting—one thinks of Ninon de Lenclos and Mistinguette." Now when I came back to Paris in the winter of 1952–1953 for the first time since 1944, I too found it exciting; but since I was engaged in driving a car across the city, I did not think of Mistinguette or of Ninon de Lenclos. Indeed, in the midst of the fury of motor traffic in those age-old streets (Baron Haussmann, who built so many of them, died about sixty years ago) I confess I did not even give any thought to the metaphor of age and decay, which seems to obsess so many contemporary Americans reporting on Western Europe; and if the image of death did cross my mind, it was not a tragic Toynbean collapse of a great society that worried me, but a simple vulgar fear for my own safety in traffic at least as dense as in the United States, and, most Americans feel, even wilder.

Now I must warn the reader that by temperament and training I am disposed to doubt the accuracy of reports like those I have just cited. By temperament I am probably a kind of optimist. At least I believe that there is a hard re-

sisting core of human nature which will stand much more
eroding from the forces of evil than it has had even in these
devilish times. By training I am a historian, and in particular a historian of revolutions in the modern West. In a
revolution the commentators, and indeed often the participants, are inclined to announce that everything that was
has been destroyed, that everything that is has become
magically new. The hurricane has blown down all the
trees; we've got to plant new ones—full-grown ones if
possible. But if you will look carefully at revolutions in the
past, you will discover some very tall oaks, to say nothing
of a thicket of less imposing vegetation, standing there
after the winds have done their worst. In the France of
1794, after five years of increasing revolutionary violence,
you will find not only the thicket of French family relations growing as before, but you will find at least one
sturdy oak of the *ancien régime,* the power of the central
government, standing stronger than ever in its new growth.

I was, then, in advance skeptical of the diagnosis of fatal
disease in the collectivity of postwar Western Europe,
skeptical of metaphors of all-destroying storms, even
though—perhaps, just because—they came from such distinguished intellectuals as Mr. Koestler and Mr. Shirer.
Six months of travel in Britain, France, Switzerland, and
Spain in the second half of 1952 confirmed me in my
belief that—to put it mildly—the condition of Western
Europe is not as bad as it is generally believed to be in this
country. This book is an effort to justify and explain that
belief.

There is indeed a certain arrogance in the famous phrase
of the historian Leopold von Ranke, a phrase which nevertheless the most relativistic of historians would hardly deny

in his heart: *er will bloss erzeigen, wie es eigentlich gewesen* —he (the historian) will merely show how it really was. But there is an arrogance, too, in the writer of the opposite sort who feels that his own emotional responses to the universe are somehow in themselves the best version of how it really is. I do indeed think that I have in this book given a truer, a more accurate account of the temper of Western Europe in our times than has, for one instance, Mr. Shirer in his *Midcentury Journey*.

I did not, of course, go to Europe with an open mind— not at any rate open in the sense in which naïve common sense seems to think of the objective scientist's mind. I did not go without guiding predispositions, without even tentative answers to tentative questions. In short, I did not go with an empty mind. I went, needled no doubt by reading men like Mr. Koestler, quite convinced that I should find more signs of life in Western Europe than of death, more signs that men and women were struggling bravely and not altogether unsuccessfully against very grave difficulties indeed than signs that they were lapsing into despairing apathy or struggling feverishly and vainly like a sick person turning from side to side—from Left to Right—in hopeless sickness. I found substantially what I expected to find, as, quite clearly, did Mr. Shirer.

What marks objective thinking, however, is not absence of expectations or even, if you like, of conclusions made in advance, but a willingness to revise those conclusions if observation and experiment fail to confirm them. I trust that if I had found in Europe that my observations, the "facts of the case," showed in the balance that my anticipations had been wrong, showed that Europe was in as bad a way—well, in almost as bad a way—as these writers I quote have said it was, I should have had the courage to revise my conclusions. Actually I found Western Europe, as far as I could pretend to judge its temper as a whole, just a shade better than I had expected to find it. But objectivity in the study of human relations is very difficult to attain, far more difficult than in the natural sciences, where the "is" and the "ought to be"—or even the "I want it to be"—get so much less in each other's way than in the study of human relations. Take this book, if you must, as no more than an emotional antithesis to the thesis of the prophets of doom and the bellyaching intellectuals.

Finally, I have not interviewed the great in those countries of Western Europe we visited, nor, in any formal sense, in the sense meant by either newspaper reporter or pollers of public opinion when they conduct an interview, have I interviewed ordinary West Europeans. We traveled quite frankly for pleasure; and indeed it seems to me no small item on the side of the thesis that Western Europe is not hopelessly sunk in despair and decay that travel for pleasure there should be quite possible. The dollar is of course an advantage; but not even in Spain, which boasts its cheapness for the American tourist, has the dollar today the shocking advantage over local currency it had in countries like Austria right after the war of 1914–1918. In the course of such normal travel I saw and talked informally with a great many people, by no means all of them engaged in the business of catering to the traveler; I saw many of my old friends in Britain and in France, friends for the most part in academic life, and not inclined to undue optimism in these days. I sampled the newspaper and periodical press in each country, neglecting neither Left nor Right. I had, as a backlog, some seven years all told of residence and travel in Europe, mostly in Western Europe, extending at intervals from 1919 to the present, and including two years of residence in London and Paris during the last war. Out of these materials, and the reading of much of the work of my fellow commentators on Europe and the modern world, and with the temperament and the training I have tried to make clear to the reader, I have made this book.

On Method, Briefly

It is certainly presumptuous to attempt to analyze the state of mind, the temper, of some three hundred million people in the Western Europe of today. Even the most confident maker of generalizations must occasionally be disturbed by the leaps in the dark his mind has to make when he works up his incomplete supply of facts—no matter how big it is, it can never in matters of this sort be complete—into general propositions. Especially in the social sciences, one ought not to be too harsh on the researcher, naïve though he may be, who sticks to his little pile of carefully assayed facts and refuses to generalize. He also serves, and in this world where the crusader (who is inevitably a generalizer of sorts) has so much to crusade for and against, it seems a waste of time and energy to crusade against the Ph.D. and kindred research, even though it is devoted to such subjects as a statistical analysis of the reading habits of eight-year-olds in Buncombe County or of learning-response among a selected group of hamsters.

For we shall always have plenty of generalizers. Indeed, the very researchers who refuse to generalize about their own work will probably feel quite confident that the big trouble with contemporary France is the lack of a two-party system like ours and Britain's. We must make generalizations, even about Western Europe, which has not the political structure of a nation-state like France or Great Britain, which is, indeed, a comprehensible group or a whole only in the much less obvious and concrete sense of sharing a certain cultural tradition. Something more than the usual semantic grace with which it is now the fashion to approach problems like the one we are concerned with here is surely necessary. For men like Mr. Shirer and Mr. Koestler are serious, honest, and most intelligent thinkers, men who have had a long experience of the Western Europe they write about. At the very least, before we attempt to criticize their conclusions, we must make some attempt to understand how they came to them, why they omitted what seem to us quite obvious and pertinent "facts," why they weave other "facts" into a distorted pattern of generalization.

The easy and really quite unavoidable thing to say is that these prophets of doom are intellectuals. Now "intellectual" is a thoroughly bad term, rousing from the start all those hindrances to understanding the semanticist deplores. But it is better than the revealing vulgarisms, from "high-brow" to "long-hair" and "egghead," Americans have coined for it, and it is better than awkward if more accurate phrases like "one whose main occupation, or at least main avocation, is writing, teaching, preaching, acting, or the practice of the fine arts." The audience for these active intellectuals I should call the "intellectual classes." I like neither term, but I am at a loss for better ones. I hope that I am trying to use these terms neither in abuse nor in praise. Most of my readers, surely, are themselves intellectuals.

Now when he is confronted with a most involved problem such as that of describing the state of contemporary Western Europe, the contemporary intellectual if he belongs to the fashionable school of prophets of doom tends to omit certain facts and emphasize certain other facts. My literary correspondent, for example, emphasizes that Paris is an *old* city. So it is. It first appears in written history almost exactly two thousand years ago as Lutetia Parisiorum. Actually archaeology does not as yet push it back much further, but two thousand years is good enough for "old." Yet surely the overwhelming majority of the artifacts that make up Paris in 1953—the streets, sidewalks, buildings, sewers, lights, the rest of the public utilities, parks, all taken together—are no older than such artifacts in our American cities. One may guess that at least three quarters of the urban agglomeration we call Paris is less than seventy years old. You have to look hard in Paris to find the Middle Ages, and look very hard to find Lutetia Parisiorum. In some obvious and surely not unimportant respects Paris is a "young" city. This my correspondent does not say, not because he does not know it to be true, but because he is not thinking in terms that make such facts pertinent to his purposes.

I do not intend to let this excursion into what is really the enormous and most important subject of the sociology of knowledge get out of hand, and quite bury the main purpose of this book. But I may suggest that a carefully balanced analysis of what can justly be called "old" and what "new" in a city or a society is likely to turn out so complicated, so much a matter of delicate shadings, that the reader gets confused. He finds the analysis dull. And the intellectual, quite laudably, hates to be dull. A complete account of how the thinker's "purposes" affect his analysis would of course be a sociology of knowledge in itself. But I do wish to bring out two habits of mind of the modern intellectual which I think are of special importance in distorting his account of matters that do directly concern this study.

Let me start with a concrete instance, which I hope will turn out to be more pertinent to our purpose than it may at first seem to be. There is in the forest wilderness of Essex County, Vermont, a small body of water known as South America Pond, to which I once struggled through the black flies. The limited view one gets from the edge I reached does not suggest that the name makes any sense; but on the map the pond does look exactly the way South America looks—*on the map*. It has that familiar shape, bulge of Brazil and all. But only a generation brought up on school geographies could have so christened the pond. Had Samuel de Champlain himself penetrated to that part of the state he is said to have been responsible for naming from its Green Mountains, he could hardly have thought of the name South America Pond. One may say that in a very limited sense the name fits, though in most of what strikes an observer—the physiographic setting, the flora, the fauna —there is no relation whatever to South America. What actually are associated in this limited valid relation are symbols—abstractions if you don't mind—not by any means fresh, immediate sense-data, the things one ordinarily notices in New England ponds. Anyone who gathered from the name that there are llamas grazing on the banks of South America Pond, or that balsa-log craft float on its surface, would be very wrong indeed.

What I am trying to illustrate thus laboriously is merely the fact that with the great expansion of what has to go into our minds about the modern world, an expansion without which we could not live at all in this world, a great deal of our thinking has to be done in terms of relating symbols to other symbols, abstractions to other abstractions. But this useful and indeed necessary kind of thinking carries with it a grave danger: that it will go on indefinitely, symbol breeding symbol, without the necessary refreshing return of the mind to the directness of sense-experience. My correspondent, his mind full of French literature and history, was no doubt justified in linking the symbol "Ninon de Lenclos" with the symbol "Paris"—but only in a very limited sense. No one who looks at Paris with his eyes instead of his literary memories and preconceptions would see it first as an aged courtesan—nor even, actually, as a young one. Paris is indeed interested in sex, but by no means obsessed with it. For Paris as for the rest of France, sex is too important to be an obsession.

The second distorting habit of mind I want to mention is much more familiar to us in these days when everyone is a psychologist. It is the inevitable coloring our emotions give to our thinking, a coloring that goes on reproducing itself, even intensifying itself. Change awakens and stimulates our emotions; it takes an effort of the mind to keep hold on what persists, maintains itself. Disaster seems to call for adjectives like "complete," "total," "unparalleled"; anything less would mark one as insensitive. Disaster can indeed be total for the individual, but here on earth, very rarely indeed for the group. When Mr. Shirer writes that the Europe he first came to in 1925 "no longer existed" in 1950, he not merely makes a statement that is true only at a certain level of abstraction, true *with respect to* unstated conditions; he also gets the pleasure—I think it *must* be a pleasure for these prophets of doom—of letting his emotions well up freely.

We must not, however, yield to the Hegel that lurks within us all and try to get at the truth by asserting the exact opposite of these gloomy views. Even in the hands of masters of paradox like Bernard Shaw and Gilbert Chesterton, the technique of maintaining that what benighted ordinary people take to be black is really shining white can get a little wearing. A good many experienced people think and feel that Europe is in a bad way, and the very existence of this opinion must for us be one of the facts of life. Some academic devil in me does tempt me to defend the paradox that the United States, not Western Europe, is old. There is a good start in the statement, true within definable limits, that in a formal sense ours is the oldest political constitution of the major states of Western society. The United States is as a formal state older than the Fourth French Republic, older than the West German or the Italian Republics; it is older than the present British semisocialist state. Or, if you like to think of Britain in terms of Alfred the Great and Magna Carta, you will also have to think of the United States in those terms. There is a more dubious follow-up in Mr. Stuart Hughes's feeling that the United States is somehow a kind of Byzantium, a society born old. I shall withstand the temptation, however, to make ours an "old" country too, and seek nothing more spectacular than a balanced account of the state of contemporary Western Europe.

II

The Urgent Present

The Extent of Western Europe

The term "Western Europe," which used to have chiefly a geographical connotation, has since 1945 taken on political and indeed moral connotations. We all use it, quite conscientiously, where in the old days we should simply have written "Europe" and let it go at that. It is true that the more than merely geographical factors that distinguish Western from Eastern Europe have existed for many years. They were not created, though they were certainly sharpened, by the events of the postwar years. Men debated whether Russia really belonged in Europe long before Yalta and Potsdam. But the Iron Curtain is no mere metaphor. Whether it divides essentially kindred if at present alienated peoples, or whether it divides peoples of irreconcilably opposed fundamental cultures—whether, in short, it is like a Mason and Dixon's line in our own ante-bellum days or like the historically shifting but very definite line that divides Christian and Mohammedan cultures from the seventh century on—it is now a very real line. The metaphor of the curtain is apt. There is indeed a curtain, which can be raised or lowered a bit, and no solid wall.

It runs, roughly, north and south along a line from the Elbe to the head of the Adriatic Sea, and then east and west to the Turco-Bulgarian frontier on the Black Sea. Like most such lines, it has its anomalies. Yugoslavia is for most purposes, though a Communist state, on the western side of the curtain; little Albania, though fronting on the Adriatic, is quite clearly on the eastern side. It has the great anomaly, that since in common language we talk of "Western Europe" as synonymous with "Europe outside the Iron Curtain," Western Europe has to stand for Southern and even Southeastern Europe, for the Iberian Peninsula, Italy, Greece, and Turkey. To get matters straight, we may list the "sovereign states" on the western, on "our" side of the curtain, with their populations and areas in round figures.

Table 1. Population and Area

	Population	Area in square miles
Great Britain	50,000,000	94,000
Republic of Ireland	3,000,000	27,000
France	42,000,000	213,000
Belgium	9,000,000	12,000
Luxembourg	300,000	1,000
Netherlands	10,000,000	16,000
Norway	3,000,000	125,000
Sweden	7,000,000	173,000
Denmark	4,000,000	17,000
West Germany	49,000,000	95,000
Switzerland	5,000,000	16,000
Portugal	9,000,000	35,000
Spain	29,000,000	196,000
Italy	47,000,000	116,000
Greece	8,000,000	50,000
Turkey	21,000,000	297,000
Total	296,300,000	1,483,000

These are rough figures, for the most part estimates made by statisticians of the United Nations for the early 1950's. They do not show the whole strength of these nations, for *as of the present* Britain, France, Belgium, and Portugal have territories overseas still tied to them by political and economic ties of varied degrees of closeness, and the Netherlands and Spain have small fragments left of their once-great overseas empires. It is not the province of this book to take up directly the complex question of the present and future of "colonialism." It is quite possible that in the long run, even in the fairly short run as history goes, European colonialism is doomed. But here, as so often when impatient prophets speak of "doom" for a politico-economic system, they take the word for the deed. Indo-China, for instance, is now almost certainly rather a liability than an asset to metropolitan France. But taking the whole network of relations gathered under the term "Europe overseas," from the tenuous bonds that hold South Africa in the British Commonwealth of Nations to the old-fashioned colonial dependence of Belgian Congo on Belgium, it is still true that overseas territories are an important factor in the total strength of Western Europe, a factor of major importance should there break out shortly a world war between coalitions headed respectively by the United States and Russia. Should such a war between the whole of the non-Communist and the whole of the Communist world break out, our side would have, in spite of the presence of thickly populated China on the Communist side, a very great advantage in population, area, and total material resources.

Our main concern in this study, however, is Western Europe itself. In the broad sense which includes the sixteen countries above listed, Western Europe has some 300,000,-000 inhabitants and 1,500,000 square miles. The USSR had in 1947, by their own government estimate to the United Nations, 193,000,000 inhabitants and 8,500,000 square miles; the United States in 1953 had just 160,000,000 in-

habitants and some 3,000,000 square miles. We shall, however, in this study be more directly concerned with the
heart of Western Europe, that part more clearly indicated
by the old geographical term "Northwestern Europe"—that
is, Great Britain, France, West Germany, and the smaller
countries of Scandinavia, "Benelux" (shorthand for Belgium, the Netherlands, and Luxembourg), Ireland, and
Switzerland. Recent events have linked Italy closely to this
area, as—at least until very recently—they have tended to
divide Spain from it. The five centuries since the great
period of geographical explorations of the fifteenth and six-
teenth centuries have made this region the richest, most
industrialized and most populous part of Europe, its heart-
land. It was not always such, and we should be usurping the
role of the prophet were we to assert that it always will be
such. For the present, however, these countries are a very
great part of Western society and civilization. Taken together these eleven countries have a total population somewhat greater than that of either the USSR (without its
satellites) or the United States.

But can they be realistically "taken together"? They are
still, in spite of the Schuman Plan, the North Atlantic
Treaty Organization, the Council of Europe, and the
United Nations, eleven independent "sovereign" nations.
Their past, even their very recent past, has seen them at war
in a great variety of combinations. Some of the great—one
almost said "classic"—antagonisms between human groups,
that between the Germans and the French, that between the
Irish and the English, and that—by no means ended though
the two have not formally fought in a declared war one
against the other since 1815—between the French and the
British, have grown up in this small area. One of our main

tasks in this book must be to examine the extent to which close political and economic coöperation, perhaps even a degree of actual union, is likely or possible in this Western Europe of the mid-twentieth century. But from the very start of our inquiry we must be warned against the over-simple formula "either–or." The problem of the 1950's is not one of either complete union of Western Europe or complete disintegration of Western Europe. It is rather how great a degree of the much-needed coöperation between the states of Western Europe is consistent with the actual state of mind—and body—of their peoples.

A Traveler's Glimpse

On the surface certainly the traveler in the heartlands of Western Europe, if he is not too bemused by the pre-conception that he is watching the death throes of a civi-lization, sees much to remind him that he is in one of the regions of the world where many men live well materially. The standard of municipal housekeeping is high, lower per-haps in France than in England or in Switzerland. But the back streets of Paris are still cleaner than the back streets of New York, and the post offices in smaller French towns are no more dismal than those in ours used to be before the New Deal muralists and architects brightened them up. The standard of domestic housekeeping remains high, higher in the poorer urban areas, in terms of what meets the traveler's eye, than in corresponding areas in this country.

The Golden Arrow still shoots at a dizzy speed across the plains of northern France, the Flying Scotsman still flies, its dining-car service a bit reduced in elegance perhaps, but no more than is fitting for the railroads of a social democracy. In Mayfair the hundreds of luxury shops make seductive displays, still with that touch unique to London that makes them even more seductive for the male customer than for the female. In Paris the *haute couture* flourishes. And neither in London nor in Paris does it appear that all the buyers are American. In French provincial towns the windows of *patisseries* and *charcuteries* are as full as ever of good things, so full that you know that ordinary Frenchmen must somehow find the francs for their *baba au rhum* and their *galantine de volaille*. No doubt the francs thus spent on delicacies cannot usually be stretched to cover electric blankets and television sets. It is indeed true that it is easy to convert to the uses of modern war factories making electrical gadgets, and quite impossible to so convert small shops making pastry, or even larger ones canning *pâté de foie gras*. It may be that the French, in thus preferring delicate foods to the products of the assembly line are, in a sense not meant by the coiners of the adage, digging their graves with their teeth. But somehow one hopes not.

No one could miss in England or France the scars of the last war, and they are of course even more visible in Western Germany, where I have not been since the war. Yet here again the eye will see what the heart wants and the mind expects. If you look for evidence that proves the last war so destructive that another war must destroy the physical basis of life where it is fought, you can find it, in London around St. Paul's, in the heart of Rouen or Beauvais and everywhere in Berlin. If you just look, however, you will see surprisingly little that will remind you of the horrors of war. The countryside has everywhere come back to its normal high state of cultivation. Indeed, this last war was so much a war of movement that almost nowhere did the countryside suffer the intensified destruction of the top-soil it suffered in 1914–1918 along the line of trench fighting. The traveler who knew his England even so recently as the 1920's will indeed see a revolutionary change, but it is not quite the kind of change that suggests death and decay. They really are using, to grow grain, sugar beets, and the inevitable potato, those lovely hedged green fields which before the war seemed to a foreign layman's eye chiefly devoted to forming a fit setting for the horseback pursuit of the fox.

They are, in spite of the demands of rearmament, rebuilding, and on a vast scale. The hopeful modernist planner must be for the most part disappointed in the results. In England and in France at least, they have not avoided stringing together long lines of houses which, if they are not now quite as ugly as the semidetached villas of the Victorians and the Edwardians, look as though in fifty years they may seem even uglier. But they have what even Americans would consider the modern conveniences; they are comfortable. There is of course almost everywhere a continuing crisis in housing. But this crisis is by no means wholly due to the destruction caused by war. It is due quite as much to a phenomenon we shall return to later, a phenomenon which surely suggests life rather than death. There are several million children in Western Europe who according to the demographic experts of the 1930's just have no business being there. Prosperous Western Europeans, like Americans, are having more babies.

There are those, both Americans and Europeans, who maintain that people in Western Europe are unhappy, and look it. M. Jean-Paul Sartre thinks that the French working-man, beaten by his natural enemies, his employers, cheated of the great hopes of the Liberation, has resigned himself to despair. A long time ago, in the most golden of golden ages, a Yankee intellectual, who was very Yankee and very intellectual, remarked that most men lead lives of quiet desperation. Thoreau's statement is not one that can be readily verified by the social scientist or even by the man of common sense. Noisy desperation, like that of M. Sartre, you can indeed verify quite easily; but quiet desperation by its very nature can be verified only in the intimacy of personal relations. I doubt whether M. Sartre has this intimate relationship with any of the workers whose cause he champions, any more than had poor old Wordsworth with the peasants he wrote about so touchingly. One of my good academic friends in Paris, forced by slender retirement pay to live in a working-class quarter, remarked to me that the workers in his neighborhood were said to be crowded ten in a room; but he admitted that since he is a bourgeois intellectual, he does not really mix with his neighbors. He had never actually *seen* them housed ten in a room—never, in fact, looked personally into their housing. As far as the superficial observation of a foreign traveler can go, I can only say that not even in Spain, where the poor really are poor and numerous, did I gather from the looks of the people that they were in either noisy or quiet desperation. The children, indeed, looked almost happy, as well as healthy, but this is perhaps an adult delusion.

Though again the social scientist has no really effective means of measuring such things, we all do register subjectively some comparative impressions of the feelings of the crowd. One of the favorite comparisons, which I suppose most of us have indulged in at one time or another, is that of the looks of our fellow passengers in subways, buses, trams. Here I am hopelessly conventional. I find a New York subway crowd the most harried, unhappy of crowds, and in their midst I come almost to believe that Thoreau was right about human beings. I find contemporary London and Paris subway crowds much less harried in appearance, and provincial busloads in Western Europe sometimes almost merry.

The traveler in Western Europe who knew the region before war broke out in 1939 will indeed be struck with one conspicuous difference from the old days, a difference reflecting the big facts the historian and the commentator chronicle. Englishmen, before 1939 and even more before 1914 a more important element in the prosperity of the great continental tourist industry than were the free-spending Americans of legend, are certainly not traveling the way they used to. Their government, whether Labour or Tory, simply does not let them have the foreign exchange they would need for continental travel. At most, by traveling on British planes and ships, and by all sorts of subterfuges even the virtuous British will indulge in for the sake of a continental holiday, a few manage to squeeze in a few weeks in the sunshine. You will indeed see them in Paris, in Switzerland, on the Riviera, in their accustomed haunts. If you have taken seriously the rhetoric of American commentators who state with beautiful simplicity that the British can no longer travel at all in Europe, you will be surprised to see so many of them. Still, there is only a trickle where there used to be a flood, and those continental Europeans who used to complain so bitterly about the demanding British, always wanting tea, baths, and food without decent sauces, are now complaining bitterly about their absence.

Exchange restrictions do indeed weigh on most nationals of Western Europe, the lucky Swiss excepted. Some of the slack in the tourist industry has, however, been taken up by travel within one's own country. The English may not be able to go abroad, but they can—and do—flock to their own resorts. They still display their great national addiction to the seaside, but they spill over into the interior. Keswick in the Lake Country in summer would shock Wordsworth and Southey, and the peak of Helvellyn is thickly peopled the moment the clouds lift, which they occasionally do. The French travel a good deal in France, in spite of, or perhaps because of, inflation.

All in all, the traveler in Western Europe in mid-century, unless he is Mr. Shirer, will feel most of the time that he is in quite familiar, even normal, surroundings. No one, it must be repeated, can fail to see the traces of the last war. They are not pleasant to see. But neither are they omnipresent, and as we shall see, they are slowly being obliterated as the peoples of Western Europe rebuild. And, unwelcome though the reflection may be to sensitive idealists, it is a fact that Western man has long been in the habit of destroying in wars and revolutions the patient and often lovely works of peace. This last war, at least, was not apocalyptic; much, much more of the accumulated architectural work of generations of Western Europeans remains than has been destroyed. The next war may destroy Canterbury and Chartres, Beauvais (hard hit, but structurally still intact, a tribute to the soundness of medieval building even at its climax of obsession with sheer height) and everything else the Middle Ages have left us; but this war most emphatically did not.

The Material Basis

But these are mere scraps of a traveler's impressions. We must come back to the general, to statistics, if we are to have a sound scaffolding for a knowledge of the temper of Western Europe. As I have already noted, the complexity and scale of our problems make this kind of abstraction absolutely essential; it is only the abuse of these methods, the exclusive reliance on long chains of deductions from initial assumptions, that need worry us.

Now the inescapable thing about the economic state of contemporary Western Europe is this: both as a whole, and in each of its constituent national units, it is "richer" right now in the 1950's than ever before in history. Two world wars and a Great Depression have in fact left even that center of war, Western Europe, materially better off than before. This is a challenging statement, and I have put it baldly. I shall shortly seek to establish it as true, and explain it. It is, however, in itself neither a justification nor a palliation of war. I confess that I make it not without a certain emotional satisfaction at confronting the prophets of doom with a fact which I know will hardly shake their pessimism. But I do not make it gloatingly. It is not directed at the moralist, not even at the tender-minded, but only at those whose moral abhorrence of war takes the form of refusing to weigh at all the evidence in the case.

The basic explanation for the material reëstablishment of Europe—apart from whatever it is in human nature or social structure that keeps men at work—is of course that our technological and economic methods enable building to keep roughly in pace with destruction. We can destroy faster and on a bigger scale than ever before but we can build faster and on a bigger scale than ever before. There is a time lag—we do not build quite as fast as we destroy; but the general proposition holds. This balance between tearing down and building up, like the somewhat comparable balance in actual warfare between attack and defense, has clearly held true up to the present. It is, like all such balances in human affairs, a very rough one, often seriously disturbed, and of course a generalized, statistical balance of no consolation to the individual who faces absolute destruction, and of no indisputable moral value to the individual who faces absolute despair.

There are those who hold that modern technology—in particular, the atomic bomb—has ended this rough general balance between destruction and rebuilding; and some of them go on to the assertion that Western Europeans know this, know that the next war will be fought in their lands, and are haunted by this fear. Both the proposition that destruction is inevitable and the proposition that ordinary Europeans are haunted, obsessed, by the fear of destruction we must take to be unproven. The first proposition I am not competent to pronounce on, and fear indeed that it is the kind of proposition that cannot be tested save empirically. The second proposition I do not find consonant with my experience of Western Europe; at any rate, this haunting fear has not prevented the haunted from working hard, regularly, and effectively to rebuild their economies. Perhaps indeed they work out of sheer desperation, but again, I don't think so. Furthermore, good observers have reported that Europeans seem for the most part less completely haunted by fear of the next war than Americans—or at any rate, than American intellectuals.

Finally, we come to my original statement that the countries of Western Europe are "richer" now than at any other time. This vague term can be broken down into all sorts of terms for which there are statistical measures available—national income, gross national product, indices of industrial and agricultural production, and the like. I limit myself to three significant sets of indices. They come from the Statistical Office of the United Nations, which, granting the uncertainties and difficulties of this sort of statistics, seems to me about the best available source.

First, indices of mining and manufacturing production for all of Western Europe: from a base of 100 in 1937, production was still only 79 in 1947 and 92 in 1948; in 1949 the base of 1937 was exceeded with 105, in 1950 with 117, in 1951 with 128. Since the population index for Europe excluding the USSR was 107 in 1950, compared with 100 in 1936, it is clear that this rise in production means also a small rise in productivity per capita.

Second, a table taken from the *Statistical Yearbook* for 1952 (Statistical Office of the United Nations, New York, 1952, pp. 90–98) which gives index numbers for manufacturing industries by separate countries. The sources vary, and some of the indices are for "general" industrial production, including mining. But they are roughly comparable, and the interested reader can go back to the sources for technical details.

Third, indices of national income *in constant prices* by certain countries: France, 100 in 1938, 106 in 1949; Netherlands, 100 in 1938, 127 in 1951; Switzerland, 100 in 1938, 128 in 1950. The comparable figures for Great Britain unfortunately use 1946 for a base with 100; but even here the index had climbed to 113 in 1950. These are figures for total

Table 2.   Indices of Industrial Production
(1948 = 100)

	1937	*1952 (March)*
Austria	112	180
Denmark	78	118
France	96	133
West Germany	——	236
Ireland	78	125
Italy	102	144
Luxembourg	100	125
Netherlands	88	127
Norway	80	122
Spain	74 (1938)	133
Sweden	67	115
United Kingdom	88	126
United States	57	115

national income; but those for per capita income also show rises for these countries. All have been corrected for inflation.

Statistics are easily overdone, but here is a final set, one which puts my general argument for Western European prosperity, or at least normality, in the least favorable light. Here are estimates of the actual daily per capita food supplies in calories for certain countries: France, prewar, 2,830, in 1950–51, 2,700; Netherlands, prewar, 2,920, in 1950–51, 3,020; Switzerland, prewar, 3,110, in 1950–51, 3,300; Great Britain, prewar, 3,120, in 1950–51, 3,080; Belgium-Luxembourg, prewar, 2,820, in 1950–51, 2,910. Though France and Britain still showed in 1950–51 slight deficits as compared with prewar days, their citizens were clearly, on an average, getting enough to eat, and these deficits have almost certainly been overcome by 1953. Incidentally, and I suppose because the human stomach has definite limits, the statistics for the United States do not here show their usual skyrocketing tendency as compared to those for Europe.

In 1950–51 our figure was only 3,233 calories, less actually than the 3,300 for Switzerland and the 3,460 for the Republic of Ireland, which is apparently the best, or at any rate the most, fed country in the world.

Now like all statistics that deal in totals and in averages per capita, these may conceal serious concrete cases of deficiencies. Notably they may conceal the fact that the poorest ten or twenty per cent of a population is actually suffering from want. I do not think the most hostile critic of the British socialist (or better, mixed) economy really thinks that the British working classes are worse off than before the war; in fact, almost everyone agrees that they are better off. British food always has been a subject about which Frenchmen, and even Americans, like to be patronizing. But the British working classes are certainly eating better, medically speaking at any rate, than before the war. They are getting more milk and more vegetables, and somewhat more meat. Nor in general can one say that these classes in the smaller democracies are worse off. A good many vocal Frenchmen think that their own working classes are worse off, and this opinion is often echoed in the United States. I can only say that after traveling some five thousand miles through France in the fall and winter of 1952–53, I did not as a mere traveler notice what seemed to me serious and extensive deprivation. And I must add that the mere traveler, unless he is really ridden by preconceptions, cannot help noticing phenomena such as serious malnutrition in a population, especially among children, as anyone who saw German and Austrian cities immediately after the war of 1914–1918 can testify.

For a final concrete evidence that Western Europe is not wholly sunk in economic decay we need not go into statistics. Everyone who has been recently in Western Germany agrees that it is humming with industry, that apparently not even Allied bombings totally destroyed industry, that what rebuilding and retooling was necessary has in fact added to Germany's industrial efficiency. It would certainly be much better in every way if the dangers of obsolescence or economic old age could be decisively overcome by somewhat less cruel and stupid methods than warfare, but the fact seems to be that industrialists have a hard time bringing themselves to scrapping plant and machinery in peacetime. Mars is less conservative than boards of directors.

Eight years after the war, then, Western Europe has made up for the actual crude economic damage it suffered. This statement does not mean that everything destroyed has been replaced—far from it—nor does it amount to the statement that war is in effect a net economic stimulus. We should be better off morally and economically—indeed, we should be better off economically just because we should be better off morally—had the war not been a necessity. But for what these statistics measure, for the gross collective wealth of Western Europe, those prophets of doom who say that modern war has been absolutely destructive, has lessened the total wealth of nations, are clearly wrong.

In an interesting article, "Europe's Invisible Brick Wall," in *Harper's Magazine* for August 1953, Mr. Peter F. Drucker recognizes the "spectacular" economic recovery Western Europe made up to about 1951, a recovery reflected clearly in the figures I have just cited. But he points out, quite accurately indeed, that with the exception of West Germany, the corresponding figures for the last two years, incomplete though they are, show a definite flattening out of the curve of production. This flattening out alarms him. It shows, he maintains, that the Western Europeans have not really learned their economic lesson properly from us Americans. By prodigious efforts they have made up for their war losses, but they show no signs that they can gear their economy to the standards of Detroit and Texas. They are still essentially conservative, still at bottom unwilling to share a greatly increased production with their working classes. We shall in later chapters return to some phases of this problem. But right here we should note that, again with the possible exception of the Germans, most European businessmen and even government planners find it hard to forget that our American new-model perpetually dynamic economy came a fearful cropper in 1929. They are still not quite persuaded that it is safe to keep up a too "spectacular" rise in the indices of production. They may be wrong. But in itself their caution is by no means a sign of failure of nerve or energy, and in the long run it is probably just as well, if Europe is to be Americanized industrially, that the process should not be too violent and too rapid.

The destruction of human lives brings up even more acutely the moral problem. It is an evil thing for one man to be killed in war. Nevertheless, we must not even here neglect the facts. There are more people alive in Western Europe as a whole today than ever before. Statistics do not measure at all the individual tragedies of war. They are not even very accurate for total deaths and permanently disabled among the armed forces. They cannot begin to measure the broken lives among the families and the friends of the dead and disabled. The last war, if it did not kill men and women beyond the power of human reproductiveness to replace them, if even in this respect it was not as much worse than that of 1914–1918 as the most alarmist thinkers, like Mr. Sorokin, had predicted, was very bad indeed. The race was spared last time an epidemic like the influenza of 1918, which killed more than were killed in action. But the wholesale murders of Jews, the uprooting of whole populations, especially in Eastern Europe, and above all the fearful portent of Hiroshima, must give the most hard-boiled realist pause.

Yet *for the particular region with which we are here concerned*, the total loss of human life was not appreciably greater, and may have been rather less, than in 1914–1918. British Empire forces lost nearly a million in the first war, and some 350,000 in the second. French casualties were 1,385,000 killed in the first war. For the second, figures cannot be very clear because of the difficulties of estimating deaths in the resistance forces, but they were much less than a million. Casualties in the German armed forces were much worse this time than the 1,808,000 in 1914–1918, probably somewhere near 3,000,000. Even if one includes civilian deaths, chiefly from enemy air bombardment, the total number of human lives lost directly because of the war in Western Europe in 1939–1945 was not greatly in excess of five or six million. Casualties—killed, wounded, prisoners— in Eastern Europe and Asia and in the rest of the world may justify the estimates released by the United States War Department on July 24, 1945, for the whole war: 60,000,-000 in contrast with 37,000,000 in the war of 1914–1918. But it must be repeated: for *Western Europe* the blood-letting was no worse than last time, and for the United Kingdom and France, it was definitely less.

If we may use a little longer the heartless language of demographic statistics, it would appear that even the Ger-

mans, in 1953, are no less numerous than before the war—
a fact which the French do not cease to point out. The
great displacement of Germans in the East has made count-
ing heads difficult and uncertain. There were, however,
according to the last census of the Third Reich in 1939,
69,032,242 people in territories then under the German
flag. The best current estimates today for both Western
Germany and Eastern Germany—and excluding Austria—
are about the same, some 70,000,000.

Once more I must insist that I am not here trying to
make a comparison between the moral and spiritual in-
cidence of the last two great wars. However such a comparison is to be made, it is not to be made by the demog-
rapher and the statistician. There remains, indeed, a
concrete and in part material and therefore measurable kind
of war damage worth a word here, for again this damage,
great though it was in the last war, by no means equaled
what the alarmists still seem to feel it must have been. I
refer to the destruction of works of art. It has been great,
and the destruction of one minor parish church of Christopher Wren's would be too much. But the artistic heritage
of the past, seen as a whole, has suffered quantitatively
nothing like complete destruction. Priceless things have
been blown to bits, but more priceless things remain. A
rapid survey of the reports confirms what we have already
noted as a mere traveler's impression.

In the first place, the "phony war" in the West allowed
the authorities time to store in safety the greater part of
the most precious paintings and sculptures in private as well
as in public hands. Something was lost in the shuffle and the
Russians seem to have been in these matters as ruthless as
conquerors used to be in the past. But in the West at least

armies seem to have been amazingly conscientious about the protection of works of art, far more so than were armies as recently as the time of Napoleon. The masterpieces of architecture cannot be moved for protection, and it is here that the heritage of the Western past has suffered its greatest losses in this war. Of the half-dozen supremely great French Gothic cathedrals none, however, was damaged as badly as was that of Rheims in the war of 1914–1918. The great Renaissance châteaux of the Loire were spared. In England the stupid "Baedeker raids" of 1942 did surprisingly little damage and all the great medieval cathedrals are basically unharmed. By great good luck the Germans at Canterbury succeeded in damaging seriously only a very frigid Victorian restoration of the library. Oxford was never bombed, in spite of its great Morris motor works— since, according to a widespread folk belief in England, Hitler had designated Oxford as his capital for the occupation, and wished it to remain intact. Cambridge too survived with no damage to its lovely colleges. The loss of many Wren churches in the City of London is indeed deplorable, but St. Paul's stood with no more than a hole in the North Transept, quite reparable, and there are still many good churches by Wren and his followers quite intact.

Nor was the damage in Italy as great as many of us feared during the war it would be. Rome was spared, as were Venice and most of northern Italy. German destruction of the approaches to the Arno bridges in Florence was a disaster, but most of Florence is intact. Battle raged right through the marvelously preserved Greek temple of Paestum in southern Italy, which many think gives the best impression of what a Greek temple was like of all now existing. Paestum is still there. In general, and in spite of the landings in

Sicily, the living record of the greatness of ancient Greece and Rome in Italy is as good as ever. Perhaps the most thoroughgoing destruction in Italy was that of the great historic monastery of Monte Cassino; but centuries of war and civil troubles, and even changes of taste, had already made Monte Cassino, however great its spiritual associations, a not very important monument of architecture.

In Germany certainly the loss for the lover of architecture was very great indeed. Berlin was a comparatively new city, and though there were no doubt those who loved it—though one must not be heartless in such matters—it was not on the whole a lovely city. But the loss of some of the most fascinating of medieval buildings, especially in Bavaria and in the heart of Frankfurt-am-Main, is irreparable, and worst of all, though since it is in the Russian zone Westerners cannot readily check the damage for themselves, is the apparent destruction of the greatest of baroque cities, Dresden. Still, once more, Germany has by no means been leveled to the ground. Much more even of the Middle Ages remains than has been destroyed, and the Germans, with their fondness for the Middle Ages and their great scholarly fund of knowledge of them, can be trusted to do a good job of restoration.

We must, however, return to the more mundane facts of contemporary European economic life. Now I do not wish to be understood as saying that all is serene on the economic front in Western Europe. The region as a whole, and its separate nation-states, are clearly not yet economically retrogressive in terms relative to their own past. Their rates of growth have indeed—as have, incidentally, such rates in New England—slowed down in comparison with some periods of the nineteenth or early twentieth centuries, but they still have dynamic economies. Their basic difficulties in a material sense stem from the fact that other parts of the world are growing faster industrially, making it more difficult for these Western European nations to sell outside their area the manufactured goods and the economic services which they have to exchange for food and raw materials to supply their dense populations. Though France at a pinch—a most unrealistic pinch that could never really come—could feed and clothe and house its millions at something near present standards wholly on the basis of internal trade, or national autarky, Western Europe as a whole has to export or give up its present standard of living. And one thing is very clear and must never be forgotten: contemporary West Europeans are used to a high standard of living, and are in no mood to accept a lower one.

Historically, Western Europe has been able to build itself up as the great center of material civilization because its particular skills in industry, shipping, finance, government, and war were greater than those of other peoples. The basic exchange—for it was an exchange, and no mere exploitation—was that of Western European finished goods and economic services for food and raw materials produced in other parts of the world. You may call those other parts of the world "colonial" if you like, and rub your hands with glee now that the colonies are getting their own back. I suspect that some centuries from now a conscientious and decently remote historian will be able to record this long process from Da Gama and Columbus to the present as on the whole the least purely exploitative, the most nearly a fair exchange, of all the prolonged contacts in the past between materially superior and materially inferior societies and civilizations. Europeans killed natives, and even snubbed them; yet somehow the natives got richer and more numerous.

But we need not draw the problem of the past of colonialism as a red herring across the trail of the problem we are engaged on. The point is that there are now in Western Europe millions of people—some fifty millions or more at a very rough guess—in excess of the number which could be maintained at their present standards of living were the area somehow sealed off from the rest of the world. But the area, in spite of the wilder prophets of doom, is certainly not now so sealed off. As I have tried hard to show, these extra men and women are still living, and not—again we speak in general terms, not in those of private lives of individuals—living in misery.

They are living as well as they are for a great number of reasons, some of which I propose to consider. Americans will perhaps think first of all, naturally enough, of the Marshall Plan and its successors. No one should minimize the importance of the aid we have brought to Europe. Indeed no one who remembers, say as an index to our former state of mind the remark attributed to Calvin Coolidge about the war debts of 1914–1918, "They hired the money, didn't they," should fail to recognize that we have, whatever our motives—and I think we can say with due understatement that they have been mixed—achieved an extraordinary change of mind and policy. But we must not exaggerate. We have not wholly supported a good-for-nothing indigent Europe. Our aid over the years has not been more than the "pump-priming" it was designed to be. It has been a marginal aid, aid which has made the crucial difference between struggling along and getting ahead.

More important quantitatively than American aid has been the fact that, again contrary to the prophets of doom, the basic relation between Western Europe and some at least of the rest of the world we can simply call the "colonial system" has not at one stroke been destroyed. Raw materials still come in to Liverpool and Marseille, Antwerp and Rotterdam, and finished goods and services still go out from them. This trade is in part still something like the old colonial trade; that is, it goes out from a mother country to a relatively undeveloped true colonial dependency, goes out from Britain, France, or Belgium to tropical Africa or to Malaya, to Madagascar or Belgian Congo. It is in part a newer development of such trade, between a European manufacturing and banking mother country to a free or partly free dependency still predominantly a supplier of raw materials. Such is the classic trade between Britain and her self-governing dominions— to which India, Ceylon, and Pakistan still belong—between France and French North Africa. It is in part trade between such European countries and "sovereign" states in various parts of the world which are still willing and able to trade their raw materials for finished goods. Trade between Britain and the Argentine, for instance, though it is not what it was in the Victorian heyday, is still a major factor in the British economy, as the recent hard-won trade agreement between the two countries should remind us.

Finally, some of this life-giving trade is of the kind that the more hopeful classical economists of the last century held would someday be the great form of international trade, exchange of their most advantageously produced commodities among fully matured balanced industrial economies. We American masters of all the material arts still do consume British jams and biscuits, British woolens, even British motorcars, French wines and other luxury goods, Swiss watches, German optical instruments and hardware, and a great deal else from all parts of Europe. We Americans still travel on foreign ships and planes, still use European financial services, and of course still spend much more as tourists there than Europeans do as tourists here. At the risk of being tedious, I must once more insist that not even the unheard-of, unprecedented revolutionary changes of our lifetime—I use the favorite language of our publicists—have totally changed the conditions of international trade. A Cobden brought back to life would certainly be deeply shocked by the world of the 1950's, but he would, if he kept his sanity, not find it wholly unrecognizable.

In short, bad as the world looks today, Western Europe can prosper economically if the world gets no worse. Europe is unlikely again to be the overwhelmingly major industrial and financial center of the world. She can, however, remain an important part of the world. But are there perhaps reasons internal to Western Europe, factors of weakness that threaten absolute instead of relative economic decline? We arrive at the most delicate point of our analysis of the economic basic of present-day Western Europe.

The central point the pessimists make is this: Generally speaking, and with exceptions here and there, especially for those marvelous people the Germans, who seem almost as gifted in technology and industrial organization as we Americans, Western Europeans cannot produce efficiently enough to compete successfully in any kind of world market we are likely to have. Their PMH—production per man hour—simply isn't high enough to compete with "younger" peoples, ourselves, the Canadians, the Japanese, perhaps even the Russians. The analysts give varied sets of reasons for this European lack of efficiency. The favorite one in American conservative circles is a simple blanket explanation: Western Europe has gone or is going socialist, with the greatest and richest nation, Great Britain, in the lead. And of course no socialist country, say the conservatives, can compete with a country where private ownership, rugged individualism, and laissez faire still prevail. Another explanation dwells on the age of European plant and organization. Europe led the world industrially, and precisely because of this fact she is now suffering from the handicaps of economic old age, obsolescent equipment, exhausted natural resources—here the British coal industry is held up as a horrid example of the multiple ills of old age—and, a rather more subtle point, a lack of willingness to experiment with new techniques and products, a drying-up of inventiveness and entrepreneurial daring, a blocking of the career open to talent, in short, psychological old age, if not senility, among the managers.

Another variant argument stresses the inability or unwillingness of the West European laboring classes to work hard and effectively; they are said to be corrupted by a socialist desire to get something for nothing, by an old-fashioned laboring-class solidarity which makes them resent a fellow worker who tries to earn more than the average, by a mistaken feeling that their employer is their natural enemy. This last is a feeling which some critics say is justified enough, since their employers have not seen the light, as American employers have, and have refused to give them the higher share of their product they need if mass industry is to work. Other economic analysts extend this kind of blame to all social classes in Europe, maintaining that industrialists, farmers, and workers are all intent on too high standards of personal consumption, that they refuse to accept that abstention from immediate consumer's goods without which not enough of the gross national product is plowed back into means of increased production, that is, capital investment. The broadest and most hopeless analysis of all adds as a final damning factor the assertion that the little peninsula we call Europe, although it had the coal, iron, climate, and other basic resources to give it the lead in the first industrial revolution, now lacks the oil, hydroelectric potential, nonferrous metals, even the sheer market area, needed to enable it to keep up with the second industrial revolution of our own time.

All this adds up to a gloomy analysis indeed, and it is tempting to agree with the economic experts both here and abroad who have come to the sad conclusion that the best that can be done for poor senile Europe is to devise the kind of considerate treatment of the patient they call "economic geriatrics." But I do not think the picture is as black as they paint it, and I propose to take up very briefly the pessimistic arguments I have just brought forward. But do not misunderstand me. I am not trying to make a mechanical rebuttal of these arguments, and come out with the conclusion that all is well in contemporary Europe. There is some truth in all these arguments, and I am trying to do no more than estimate the degree of truth they have.

The least sound I believe is the ecological argument that

Europe has not got the resources to maintain a reasonable degree of prosperity in our neo-technical age. It is true that there is almost no oil in Western Europe, and that many of the regions with a great economic past, notably Britain, Benelux, and Germany, haven't the kind of rivers that can be harnessed to provide great hydroelectrical power. But the one safe generalization about technology is that it is always changing, and that it is quite impossible to predict its future. It looks to a layman as if we were on the verge of a third industrial revolution, in which the key factor will be, not coal nor oil nor water power, but sun power or perhaps atomic power. Unless indeed we cannot get beyond the very scarce uranium, which seems unlikely, it would seem that Europe starts with as high a potential in atomic power—apart from human factors of industrial and political organization—as the rest of the world. If we are to run on sun power, the future looks gloomy for the British Isles; but even there the sun shines more than American folklore will let it. It is indeed true that Western Europe is at present too politically subdivided to provide the large free market area that the most efficient modern industrial organization requires; but to this problem of breaking down present political and economic barriers in Europe we must return later in this study.

In itself, the reproach of "socialism" seems to me almost pointless. All Western nations, including the United States, are in 1953 so far from the theory, and even the practice, of classical economics, the economics of the Manchester School, that the conscientious present-day follower of the school—there are a few left, for principles die hard—must feel that all nations are almost equally far from the right way. It would be interesting but most unscientific to try to rank Western countries along a simple numerical scale like a thermometer, between a freezing point marked "socialism" and a boiling point marked "capitalism." One would need for each country a number of criteria, extent of actual nationalization of industry, actual recruitment and reward of managers, size and efficiency of industries, degree of monopoly or oligopoly in various industries, degree of government regulation, and many more. I strongly suspect that the United States would by no means come out close to the capitalism of the classical economists. On a simple centigrade scale from the zero of socialism to the 100 of capitalism, I hazard the crude guess for the United States of 60, for Britain of 40, with France at 70 and Western Germany somewhere in between the United States and Britain.

This is of course very crude guessing indeed, and I am probably basing my guess rather strongly, not so much on criteria of public or private ownership, as on the contrast between real individual ownership and managership on the capitalist side and impersonal ownership separated from bureaucratic management on the socialist side. Let me be concrete once more. I have recently been involved in a relation, perhaps even a quarrel, with an enormous department store, a relation which started with a mere misspelling of my name on their accounts. Before I got through, all the smear words of the capitalist attack on socialism—red tape, bureaucracy, irresponsibility, impersonal hugeness, general snafu—rose to my mind, and were not always successfully suppressed. I suggest that it is not by ideas about private initiative and government ownership that differences in modern economic organization of states are to be measured, but in the actual structure and practice of

economic life. If this is so, the X and Co. with whom I
quarreled is much more comparable with a government
bureau here or in Europe than with the X and Co. of the
old merchant prince who founded it in the nineteenth
century. The difference between the store of the merchant
prince and the store today is by no means wholly one of
size, though size is certainly important; it is also a difference
in the spirit and methods of management, in the way the
whole staff is trained and held together. It's as good a store
as it ever was, but of course it's not as efficient as it used
to be, in part because they are trying so damned hard to
be efficient.

This brings me to what I consider the really important
element in the pessimistic analyses of European economic
conditions I have been trying to correct. This is the assertion that the West Europeans can't keep a dynamic
economy going because they haven't the right spirit, the
right temper, to work hard enough, the assertion that they
prefer butter not only to guns, but to machine tools. With
the technical economic argument that Western Europe as
a whole consumes too much and invests too little I am not
enough of a specialist to deal competently. I do, however,
note that the economic doctors disagree on this matter,
both as to diagnosis and as to remedy, and I incline to the
belief that the patient will survive. For Europeans, whether
from climate, schooling, religion, economic necessity, or
just plain habit, have been good sound disciplined workers
for centuries, and *as a group* couldn't possibly stop for long
being such workers, even if a cosmic Santa Claus suddenly
brought them all they needed to live on. Impatient American travelers sometimes notice British workingmen knocking off for tea—and indeed at any hour of the day it would

be hard not to find someone in Britain knocking off and
brewing tea. But these Americans have apparently never
noticed American workingmen, following the advertise-
ments as like good Americans they should, pausing for the
pause that refreshes. Of course the automatic coke machine
over in the corner by the rest room is neater and more
efficient than any way of making tea—that water for tea
just has to be boiling. But I must say I was much impressed
with the polished chromium tea wagon they rolled in for
elevenses in a great Piccadilly motor firm. The young lady
who rolled it in looked like Miss Piccadilly 1952.

There is indeed a difference in tempo in the way we
work and the way West Europeans work, but it is not an
enormous, not a fundamental difference. The really central
thing is the relation between workers—including farmers—
and employing and government classes. If it is true that
French workers hate their employers, if it is true that
British workers want complete nationalization, if it is
true even generally and more vaguely that European
workers feel put upon by their bosses, then prospects will
be bad until these conditions improve. For you cannot run
a modern economy effectively very long if the class struggle
is a clear, simple, and intense conflict between workers and
employers. I do not think conditions in France, let alone
in the rest of Western Europe, are as bad as that. But I do
think that we could help Europe most if we could somehow
export to them, not just goods or even industrial technology, but some of the art of softening the class struggle,
of satisfying the human side of industry, which to the
indignation, indeed frank disbelief, of the old-fashioned
American liberal we really seem to have developed in this
country. Meanwhile, there is one hopeful concrete index

which may indicate no more than that Europe is in some kind of a boom period, no mean thing in itself, not in itself a cause for tears: almost everywhere the number of production hours lost in strikes is less, often a great deal less, than before the last war.

As I write, in mid-August of 1953, France, in any reckoning one of the key•countries of Western Europe, is indeed in the midst of a very serious wave of strikes, political rather than purely economic in purpose. They were set off by Premier Laniel's attempt to arrest inflation by reducing wages. They were greeted in the American press by the usual chorus of disapproval which we nowadays voice so freely in commentary on the efforts of our partners of 1778 to work out a viable democracy. We should, of course, be a bit more tactful and considerate, if only because we ourselves seem not yet to have been entirely successful in our efforts to stop our own milder but very real inflation by the opposite process of increasing wages. To the historian, M. Laniel's problem, and his basically conservative solution, are strongly reminiscent of Poincaré's at least temporarily successful effort to save the franc in the mid-twenties. There is indeed no guarantee that he will be even as successful as was his predecessor. Indo-China is a worse running sore than was the occupation of the Ruhr. The French middle classes are weaker than they were in the mid-twenties, the French working classes more angry, perhaps more revolutionary. At this writing it would take a very rash prophet indeed to assert that the crisis will end with a stable France and a stable franc. Yet the basic economic position of France is a sound one. The country is not, like Britain, Benelux, and West Germany, so completely industrialized as to be almost wholly at the mercy of export trade. The French have an economy well balanced between industry and agriculture, at bottom a modest economy, based on relatively small enterprises, that cannot give them anything like world-leadership, but that can give them the material basis for a flourishing civilization. They may indeed be on the point of throwing all this away in a series of disastrous class struggles with no one the victor. But once more the historian will be cautious, for he knows the history of France is full of crises which might have, but did not, destroy state and society. The modern French in particular have for many generations refused to behave in politics the way their Anglo-Saxon critics on both sides of the Atlantic have thought—and announced firmly and freely—they ought to behave. They have not, at least since 1789, been decent, quiet, and stable, like the British; *their* strikers do not play soccer with the police, as it is said the British strikers did in the general strike of 1926. It is true that French strikes are not quite as bloody as ours used, until quite recently, to be. But this fact simply points up the more fundamental fact that nations come even further than do individuals from seeing themselves as others see them. The French have been almost as violent and quarrelsome in politics as we Americans—but they have not had a fine empty continent to quarrel in. Even so, they have hitherto stopped short of self-destruction. They have made the necessary compromises, and the safest bet is that they will do so again.

To sum up: Western Europe today, despite the destruction caused by the two wars of our time, has more people and a greater total wealth than at any time in the past. It faces grave problems indeed, problems in part economic.

But they are even more problems of the kind I have tried to suggest in my title for this book, "The Temper of Western Europe." They are problems involving the whole nature of man, *homo sapiens*—and perhaps his ambivalent other self, *homo stultus*—but certainly not of that quite imaginary creature, *homo oeconomicus,* in whom the economists themselves seem to have given up belief nowadays. To some of the abiding factors in these problems, to the persistent past, we must now turn.

III

The Persistent Past

Rebuilding

In spite of the horrors of the last thirty years, the total material wealth of Western Europe is, as I have pointed out in the last chapter, greater now than ever before. Much of that wealth is a heritage of the past. I turn to the past here, not for its own sake, but because so much of the past is inevitably the present. The interplay in human affairs between past and present to make the future, between habit and invention to push us along in changing but never unprecedented ways, comes out nicely in the problems of reconstruction of the war-torn cities of Europe. In London the lovers of the past would restore every little lane in that fearfully devastated region around St. Paul's, put back every Christopher Wren church, whether or not it had any parishioners; the planners, the lovers of the future, however, would actually pull down a few buildings spared by the bombs, and have a fine uninterrupted green park going right down to the Thames. Already the extremists on both sides have lost, but I think it pretty clear that the British "middle of the way" will turn out to be pretty far over toward the side of tradition, as usual. We shall have Paternoster Row again.

The city of Tours in France seems to me an even better

illustration of the point I am trying to make, for its restoration balances past and future neatly, with French *mesure*. There was not much *mesure* in its destruction. The center of the city was bombed and burned out by the Germans, along with so many of the crossings of the Loire, in those terrible June days of 1940 when the French army was still in being—and in retreat. Allied bombing in 1944 added to the destruction. Rebuilding has been going on steadily since the end of the war. They are not restoring the maze of streets of the old city, though they are restoring the churches and one fine Renaissance house. They are building pleasant squares and moderately wide streets, though still not quite wide enough for perfect car parking in the days to come. They are building according to plan in an inoffensive if undistinguished style which looks roughly like later French eighteenth-century building stripped of most of its ornamentation.

The influence of the past, and the tough persistence with which the human race goes on giving the lie to the prophets of doom, comes out especially in the treatment of the bombed-out shopkeepers of Tours. Anyone even mildly addicted to planning anywhere in the West would be delighted to diminish the number of retail shops, which are wastefully numerous and inefficient. The new Tours surely could get along with fewer tobacconists, fewer cafés, fewer newsdealers and booksellers, fewer equivalents of our American gift shoppes. But clearly it won't. Every little bombed-out shopkeeper felt he had a right to keep on, and the government at once began building temporary wooden huts along the wide boulevards spared destruction. There you still find the shops, the crowds as lively as ever about them, doing business in the old determined, inefficient way.

As the new buildings are finished, in go the shopkeepers on the ground floor, christening the bright new quarters with flowers and champagne, and one more set of temporary wooden buildings can be torn down. The new Tours will, I suspect, have substantially the same ratio of retail shops to inhabitants as the old—perhaps indeed a slightly larger one, since the motorcar in France is doing what it has done here, in the United States, weakening the smaller local centers of retailing and building up the larger ones.

Nationalism

Certain elements in European life persist, like the shopkeepers of Tours, in spite of the blows of fate and the promises of the planners. The first of these is national patriotism. For a long time now the term "nationalism" has had generally unfavorable connotations among intellectuals and the intellectual classes in the West. Even in France, where Charles Maurras may stand as the pure intellectual reduced to the absurd, his "integral nationalism" never commanded the allegiance of more than a minority of the French intellectual classes. We find it hard to realize that once, in the days of Mazzini and his peers, national patriotism was on the side of the angels, on the side of progress, liberalism, democracy. Most of us do indeed know that Marx has been proved wrong in thinking that the working classes of the West would soon be tied together with a cosmopolitan class-consciousness far stronger than their feeling toward the political state to which they belonged. But we still have as a kind of hangover from Marxism and other forms of rationalism a belief that somehow nationalism got invented about 1789 and has been

GARDNER WEBB COLLEGE LIBRARY

foisted as a kind of opium of the people on human beings who might otherwise now all be happy citizens of the world. To many of my friends in the movement for some kind of world government, nationalism seems a fake, an illusion, an argument brought up by misguided people like me, but nothing that can't be destroyed, or at least tamed into something merely cultural, with a few strokes of the pen when the right people sign the Constitution of the World. Nationalism, at least in the sense of traditional insistence on political independence or sovereignty of the political unit, they say, makes no sense in our modern world of atomic bombs and large-scale production. A sovereign France does not make sense: therefore there really is no sovereign France.

I am of course caricaturing their position, but caricature is, one hopes, one of the possible roads to truth. The thoughts and feelings of millions of men and women, which we sum up so coldly and abstractly as nationalism, are the facts—the clinical material, if the figure of speech does not offend you too much—which we ought to try to understand before we deal with them on too large a scale and too radically. Let us take France, since to use France as an example of nationalism seems to come natural to Americans. We might indeed take the United States as an example, but there are probably good psychological reasons why we don't. A great deal of the past, before 1789 as well as after it, has gone into making most Frenchmen proud of being French, sharing in the "pooled self-esteem" of the living and the dead, and not taking orders from non-Frenchmen. As Professor Hayes has shown, France is a "nation of patriots" in part because educators, lawmakers, publicists, pressure groups of all kinds have worked so hard and so long to make it so. But the point is that such work cannot be undone at all quickly. Indeed, in the study of human affairs the familiar opposition of nature and environment is for pressing current problems altogether meaningless. It does not at all matter whether French nationalism grew spontaneously or was deliberately implanted by a scheming few. It is there, now, to be reckoned with.

Perhaps we Americans in particular underestimate the strength of nationalism in other peoples because, like the French of the great Revolution and Napoleon, our own nationalism is so firmly universalist, so almost innocently missionary in spirit. We feel sure that the rest of the world really would like to be Americans. We cannot easily understand, without a great effort at detachment and sympathy, that whole side of nationalism which stems from being, or having been, underdog, a status which at one time or other in the last five hundred years most European nations have suffered in. Southerners in this country should be able to understand that defeat makes the heart grow fonder, but among the many astonishing things about America is the fact that we do seem to have followed the "road to reunion" right to the end. A distinguished Spanish scholar, who knows his separatist Basques and Catalonians at home, is said to have had great difficulty in understanding why the Confederacy never tried it again. "Why," he said, "in my country they keep right on trying every generation or so."

I do not wish to be understood as maintaining that nationalism remains unchanged as a kind of ruling passion in the Western European countries. There are forces—but I lapse in jargon, there are real live human beings—working to transcend nationalism there. To them I shall return in a final chapter. But these people are working against others who have not yet gone far enough beyond nationalism. There are strong groups, such as the Gaullists in France and the reviving nationalist groups in Germany, for whom the nation *must* be sovereign. In Britain there are not only corresponding groups, essentially Tory in outlook, who wish to preserve the old sovereignty, but there are also many in the Labour party who feel that if Britain must somehow be integrated into a wider political community, that community must be found in closer ties within the Commonwealth or even with the United States, rather than with Western Europe.

It is almost certainly true that the old aggressive nationalism, that of Barrès, of Kipling, of *Deutschland ueber Alles*, is a much diminished faith, held only by unreconstructed fractions of the population, and even in Germany not worth the alarm they arouse in some of our American commentators. Nationalism among the many is perhaps no more than a kind of hangover, a habit, visible as a kind of distrust of foreigners, a normal parochialism of outlook. I know that many American travelers return from Europe with the feeling that, especially in France but also in Italy and in England, there is an active hatred of the United States, a kind of Americanophobia. Such travelers I think are unduly impressed with the profusion of inscriptions like "Americans, go home" and "Ridgeway la peste" which they see all over France, which are the work of an organized Communist minority in a country where Communists are still free to indulge in that kind of propaganda. Their opponents, who are I think stronger, are free to counter with inscriptions like "les Stalinistes à Moscou." Certainly many

European intellectuals are hostile to us, and it is the intellectuals who are most articulate. I do not think active hatred for the United States goes very far in the general population, not even in France. For what subjective impressions are worth I can only report that I did not feel this hostility toward myself as an American in 1952 any more than I had in the 1920's—not at least among the ordinary people a traveler meets.

It is sometimes held that nationalism is less strong, less of an obstacle to political integration, in the smaller than in the larger nations. This is true only in the very restricted sense that small countries like Belgium or Switzerland cannot possibly play the role of aggressor that Spain, France, Germany, and certainly overseas, Great Britain, have played at various times in modern history. But almost everyone who has worked for any kind of political or economic integration in contemporary Europe will tell you that the Swiss are about the hardest nuts to crack. It is not that the Swiss are wholly uncoöperative; they are up to a point good internationalists, as their history has made them. But they have stopped at about 1900. They seem to have made a fetish of their neutrality, and their feeling that this neutrality must be guarded at all costs has been, not unnaturally, strengthened by a guilty conscience. Their admirable democracy has twice within a lifespan done no fighting in defense of threatened democracy. They are not sure they can ride out a third storm, but they cannot—and for this I am sure we should not blame them—quite bring themselves to give up the old ways of neutrality that have carried them safely through two great storms. Even in the Low Countries, the efforts to bring Holland, Belgium, and Luxembourg together in "Benelux" have run up against serious obstacles. Irish nationalism is not now at the fever heat of 1921. Only a handful of Irish extremists would still like to sink under the waters of the North Sea the main island of Britain. But the Irish are always touchy. They could not quite take the recent Coronation in the fine spirit of vicarious enjoyment serenely republican America took it, but had to pretend the Coronation was none of their business. Irish nationalism still runs pretty high, and seems unlikely to abate to a level that will bring the Irish Republic to give up "sovereignty" until the problem of Ulster is somehow solved.

Political Forms

The past, certainly the immediate past of half-a-dozen generations, persists most conspicuously in political forms. In the broadest possible area Western Europe can be made to cover, that of all Europe outside the Iron Curtain, the nineteenth century had introduced and in part acclimatized some form of parliamentary democracy. Perhaps, since democracy is so complex a cluster of ideas, we may content ourselves with a rather simpler cluster, and say that Europeans by 1914 were used to the practice of *government by discussion*—discussion in the open, with individual risks in the support of radical stands greater in some countries than others, but well short of the risks of totalitarian suppression. In Spain and Portugal, though I do not think conditions come near those of the late George Orwell's *1984,* it is certainly stretching the point to say that there is nowadays true government by discussion. But everywhere else in Western Europe the old ways of talking and writing it out in public have survived two generations of prophets who kept insisting we must all agree, and what is more important, some very thorough attempts to enforce one-party unity and all that goes with it.

If widespread public acceptance of the fact that human beings have different opinions and tastes—even, indeed above all, on very lofty matters—is as I believe one of the most important elements in democracy, then it is a fact that democracy is still firmly rooted in the area with which we are here concerned. The basic fact is accepted multanimity, diversity of opinion on high matters. That multanimity in the English-speaking countries is accommodated somehow in two or three national political parties; elsewhere in the free world it may need a dozen or more, with splinter parties constantly breaking off from them. It is a difficult question how far the two-party system may be considered the normal healthy form of democratic national government and how far the multiparty system may be considered a pathological condition. With very few interludes, France has been in this latter condition for about one hundred and sixty-four years, which seems a long time for a really diseased organism to last.

The newspapers keep bringing us reminders that parliamentary government on the continent is not what it is among us happy heirs of Magna Carta. French governments fall like ninepins, and each time the pin boys seem to have a harder time setting them up again. De Gasperi is out in Italy, and Adenauer is not safe in Germany. Here again we cannot in a study of this scope attempt to go deeply into a problem that needs the most careful and considerate attention from Americans. It is a very serious problem indeed, and one which I have perhaps permitted myself undue levity about in my last few phrases. Yet it must be insisted that the approach of many of our American commentators on continental political forms is of a piece with their general attitude of gloom and horror at the failure of the universe to go the way Mr. Jefferson apparently hoped it would. Continental European democratic governments, like ours and those of the British Commonwealth of Nations, get along from day to day by a most complex balancing among the demands of all sorts of competing interest-groups. It is an undue oversimplification, but not a fundamental error, not a misleading generalization, to put the matter this way: the Europeans balance their group interests through the mechanism of the multiparty system, and we and the British balance ours through the mechanism of two parties each of which is a congeries of diverse interests. (This is especially true of the United States.) The compromises are made at different points in the working of the two systems, but the compromises are there in both. We make ours in preëlection conventions, caucuses, and above all in the push and pull of legislative committees and in the famous negotiations between the White House and Capitol Hill. These negotiations, by the way, seem sometimes to go almost as badly, to exhibit almost as much unwillingness to make decent compromises, as do the negotiations among continental parties during a ministerial crisis. The Europeans, and most conspicuously the French, make their compromises in the white light of such ministerial crises.

After all, it is hard not to grant Pope's famous couplet:
For forms of government let fools contest;
Whate'er is best administer'd is best
at least the status of a half-truth. Perhaps our system is, if judged by the standards of political science, a better system

than the European. One can go too far in relativism in this as in other matters. Yet we Americans are still such good children of one phase of the eighteenth-century Enlightenment that we tend to the quite opposite error of assuming that there is a technically best engineered model in politics as in, say, the airplane, and that this model ought to work just as well in one country as in another. The important point is inescapable: in a democracy issues among interest-groups must be threshed out in public, and they must somehow be reconciled in political action. If they cannot be reconciled, no political machinery will make reconciliation possible, as we ourselves found out in 1861. The French machinery of government did survive the very great crisis of the Dreyfus Case early in this century. If the French really want to make their democracy work, they can do so even with the imperfect machinery of the Fourth Republic. We are back, as we have been before, at the root question of the temper of a people. If the French, and other Western Europeans, really are divided, something as we were in 1861, into two great groups essentially in a state of civil war, there will have to be a civil war, or at any rate a seizure of power by some group using nondemocratic methods. But it is the thesis of this book that not even France, not even Italy, is at the moment so divided. But it is surely touch-and-go. Any very great shock to the still precarious material basis of West European life may well see an eclipse of democracy in one or more countries. But the fault will lie deeper than mere political machinery. The existing machinery, with all its faults, has proved in the past that it can provide a framework for the necessary, the grave and difficult compromises, on which democracy depends.

What I have been emphasizing in this discussion of Western European internal political structure is the persistence of that structure in the separate countries. This persistence is of importance, first because it seems to me a persistence of ways of living essentially democratic and second because it seems to me to make crystal clear that any future European political union will have to allow for a very great amount of national autonomy. These separate parties are all so rooted in their own countries that it seems impossible to merge them at first into what might be called European parties. This I believe to be true even where as with Catholic or old-fashioned socialist parties there is an apparent solid basis in ideas for getting beyond national political habits.

The fact of this political persistence hardly needs establishing here. Even where, as in West Germany and in Italy, we have witnessed something like a "restoration," a restoration which like the well-known Bourbon restoration in 1814 was in part at least imposed from the outside by victorious enemies—even in these once-fascist countries I am struck by the survival of old political ways. To the extent that these countries even before that great divide, 1914, were but marginally democratic, I think they remain marginally democratic. If you share the habits of thought of most American intellectuals, this statement will mean to you that those horrid Nazis and Fascists have been stupidly or wickedly allowed by somebody in responsible position to survive and revive, and that now it is too late. If you can approximate in these matters the relative detachment of the scientist, you will simply recognize that in human relations there is a complex set of phenomena most incompletely understood but which tend toward persistence, which have a kind of inertia. You will then recognize that in Germany and in Italy there are democratic survivals as well as totalitarian survivals, and that the fight still goes on.

But in France you find the neatest confirmation of the fact that in the ways of politics that tired, cynical but somehow not altogether discouraging folk-paradox holds true: *plus ça change plus c'est la même chose.* Nothing is quite so much like the Third French Republic as the Fourth. Party organization, party leadership, party journalism, even the details of parliamentary procedure are today substantially what they were twenty years ago. A lot of earnest and very able people tried hard after the Liberation of 1944 to mold France anew, and the fact that they encouraged the use of the locution "Fourth Republic" is a measure of their failure to effect real economic and spiritual changes. But again, we are not for the moment evaluating, nor even attempting to explain, but simply noting this persistence of the past. And here the persistence confronts with unusually simple irony the really grandiose claims to innovation made by the change from Third to Fourth. Indeed, I should think that almost any reflective person, political scientist or not, would come after reasonable study of the facts involved to the conclusion that the New Deal and the Fair Deal have changed the American Republic between 1932 and 1952 more fundamentally than the French Republic has been changed in those same years. Just to be provocative, I suggest that if we had the French habit of numerotation in these matters we should now be in the Fifth American Republic, the "revolutions" having come under Jefferson, Jackson, Lincoln, and Franklin Roosevelt.

At any rate, the past persists in European politics, and conditions the present. It is precisely on these bits of

political machinery that the sentiments as well as the
interests of men fasten, and by so fastening keep them
working, even though they work poorly, even though
blueprints for much better machinery are at hand. Nor
is it just the selfish vested interests of the few who hold
place, who run the machinery, which accounts for this
persistence. Let me take an American instance familiar to
all, and one in which no in-group feeling at all comparable
to nationalism in intensity accounts for persistence. Our
minor civil subdivisions, counties in most of the country,
towns in New England, are affronts to reason and efficiency. I bring up the phrase "horse-and-buggy" and
leave it at that.

Now the easy explanation of why we keep horse-and-
buggy counties in these days of jet planes is that the
officeholders want to keep them for purely selfish reasons.
No doubt the vested interests of the officeholders is a
factor, but surely not even in Georgia, where the counties
are so numerous, nor in rural New England, where the
towns are so numerous, are local officeholders a majority
of the population. If the people of Georgia or of Vermont
very much wanted fewer and more efficient local government areas they could get them. Perhaps it is mere inertia
that prevents reform. But when you fall into that almost
automatic "mere" you are gravely underestimating a very
important thing. Real reform is of course possible, and in
the field I am using for illustration it is being achieved. In
a field the American people really do feel strongly about,
education, we have already gone far to eliminate in favor
of the central rural school a horse-and-buggy institution,
the little red schoolhouse, which had behind it some strong
emotions other than those I have summed up as inertia. I

shall try to show later that this apparently local instance is
not without bearing on the much wider problem of
European unity.

The Persistent Social Structure

We are perhaps more prepared to accept the persistence
of the past in social rather than in political structures. Yet
even in this field a lot of Americans, and even Englishmen,
seemed to believe that in 1945 the British "revolution by
consent" was about to bring complete social equality to
England, about to eliminate the distinction between gentlemen and others. I need hardly insist that there are still
gentlemen in England. Most certainly there has been
throughout Western Europe for several centuries a process
summarily to be described as leveling, a squeezing together
of the social pyramid—better, the socio-economic pyramid
—both from top and bottom. This process has been very
much hastened in the last two or three generations, but a
pyramid remains, and not the nice straight line which one
might take as the graphic representation of the ideal of
the classless society.

Status is in our Western society a very subtle thing, and
one which varies so much among the constituent states of
this society, and indeed within each state, that only the
partly intuitive understanding of the native, the member
of the state, can grasp it. European visitors to the United
States see readily enough that ours is indeed a stratified
society, but they very often make the mistake of thinking
that the principle of stratification is wholly economic, that
in America a man is measured wholly by his wealth; and
they compound their error by assuming the untrammeled
operation of the career open to talents. Some Americans

appear to make the same mistake, in spite of Middletown, Yankee City, and a host of other places our anthropologists and sociologists have shown to be by no means societies stratified by income alone.

Like so many of the topics we have had to touch upon here, this one of social status in Western society is far too big to receive proper treatment in a brief survey. I think I can best make the point I wish to make, that of the persistence of the past, if I limit myself to the two countries I know best, two countries which if they by no means exhaust the variety of Western European social structure, are at any rate quite typical. But I do not wish to claim exemption from the limitation I have just set up. I am neither an Englishman nor a Frenchman, and I have by no means the intuitive knowledge of their societies a native would have. Mine is an outsider's view.

Victorian England, a society for which Bagehot found the searching epithet "deferential," is indeed—I was about to fall into the easy stereotype and write "dead," but of course the metaphor is a bad one. Let us say that contemporary Elizabethan England is in many ways very different from Victorian England. I find a neat concrete illustration of the change in a great English estate now freely open to the public. The park is perhaps a little less meticulously gardened than in the time of the present earl's grandfather, but the castle, the lawns, and the oaks are still there, and still splendidly Victorian. Only, the castle has been divided up into apartments for workers in a nearby city, who go in by bus. The medieval courtyard is full of modern children, bicycles, and the whole apparatus of family life. His lordship, when he is not in London, lives in what used to be the gatekeeper's lodge.

The statistics confirm the isolated instance. The almost incredible income taxes—ninety-five cents on the dollar at the top levels—and the death duties have destroyed the economic basis of these great estates. I have throughout this study sought to emphasize, as against the exaggerations of the alarmists, the fact that in human affairs change is never as complete as it appears to these alarmists to be. But of course change is real. Indeed, one conspicuous change between, say, 1850 and 1950 is that in 1850 it was the optimists, not the pessimists, who held the floor with their exaggerations. But we are concerned here with the present. One specific piece of statistics is most eloquent. Just before the last war some 7,000 individuals in Great Britain had a net income after taxation of £6,000 or over, already a very great relative lopping off of the top of the economic pyramid as compared with Victorian times. But after nine short years, in 1946, those 7,000 individuals had been reduced to 45. And meantime the pound had somewhat depreciated in value.

If the great fortunes and the great estates are gone in Great Britain, there are abundant signs of the continued existence in something short of dire straits of a prosperous upper class or gentry. Many of them will complain bitterly about the servant problem, about taxes, about currency restrictions which keep them from continental travel. But Mayfair is peopled by them, supported by them; and between Mayfair and Islington or Poplar the social distance still greatly exceeds the geographic. There are those who hold that the British upper and upper middle classes are for the most part living off capital, and that their disappearance has merely been delayed. No doubt many individuals in this class are living off capital, but I think it is clear that the "mixed" economy of Britain provides still an adequate base in executive and professional salaries, in business profits, in return on capital—remember that none of the nationalized industries was confiscated, and that the old owners are still being paid off—to support these people, if not in the style to which they were accustomed, at least in a style that will for some time mark them off as a privileged class.

One can make a long list of British ways that have not vanished in this world quite as fast as they should have vanished had the revolution of 1945 measured up to what was then written and said about it. In the cathedral close at Wells or Salisbury you can believe that Bishop Proudie is still alive; and you know quite well that Mrs. Proudie is. Nor is this survival an illusion. I am quite aware of the traps prose fiction has for the historian and sociologist. The historian of A.D 3000 who concludes from our twentieth-century American "Westerns" in fiction and in movies that the West of 1950 is still the West of 1850 will make a mistake—but, by the way, not nearly as great a mistake as our own contemporaries who believe that East, West, North, and South have now been merged in one great uniform lump. Trollope's Barsetshire, I conclude quite without irony, is still on the map.

Perhaps the public school, which sometimes seems to Americans to belong to the same level of being as Barsetshire, will serve better as an example. Many of my British friends in wartime were quite sure that whatever else survived the Labour party victory they were sure was coming, the public school would have to go. Or if the grounds and buildings were too valuable to turn over to other uses, at least the school itself would be changed beyond recognition, opened to all classes, cleansed of snobbery, modernized in curriculum. That program still exists on paper and in the minds of the New Fabians, but I do not think anyone will seriously maintain that much has been done to achieve it. I should guess that of all the Victorians, the great schoolmasters brought magically back to life today would find the little world of their profession most unchanged. Certainly Arnold would feel more at home in Rugby than Cobden in Manchester or Carlyle in Chelsea.

These are, however, details. The public school does bring up the central general problem: are there signs that the temper, the goals, the methods of the ruling class in Britain are changing? This problem is much too big for us here. But I should like to suggest that this class will survive those who have buried it in words. It has from Tudor times on showed, in contrast with most continental ruling classes, an extraordinary ability to absorb able men from lower classes, and what is even more uncommon, to slough off in the course of a few generations its most incapable members. Above all, it has managed to take in good time ideas and programs from intellectuals without ceasing to feel quite superior to intellectuals, and indeed distrustful of them. The distrust, however, has rarely degenerated into hatred, as in parallel circumstances it seems rather ominously to be doing right now in the United States. The old managers and the new planners may yet pull Britain through in a rather odd and very British partnership.

France is at least as complex a whole as Britain, and, in spite of much that we two great heirs of the Enlightenment of the eighteenth century have in common, rather harder for an American to get at intuitively. Yet even the superficial observer who knew something of the France of the Twenty Years' Truce—and earlier—can see how much of the older France survives in 1953. It is true that, though the fact has somehow not been as well publicized as the British "revolution by consent," there has been a leveling process in France in the last few generations which has made that country, too, a welfare state. It is almost as hard to keep up a great country estate in France as in England; the French upper and middle classes, contrary to a notion unfortunately widespread in the United States, are heavily taxed. It is the peasant who commonly dodges the income tax, in part at least. The taxes go not only to rearmament, but to social services, among which are relatively generous family allowances and child-welfare services which may help to justify my subjective impression that French children, though like American children they may ultimately suffer from having been objects of child worship (may I coin the word *pedolatry?*), look nowadays particularly healthy and happy.

What I wish to emphasize here is that France, though undergoing the leveling process apparently universal in Western society, preserves something of her old and very complex social stratification. Like us, and unlike the British, Frenchmen have committed themselves in the high regions of political faith to the proposition that all men are created equal. Many more in France than in America do indeed question that faith, but in both countries equality has sunk into the common ways beneath the noble beliefs. All Frenchmen are "Monsieur" just as all Americans are "Mac" or at least "Hey, you." I sometimes feel none of us will live to see the day when all Englishmen are, with the small "s," "sir." In France this equality, which is, as

I have suggested by my illustration, an equality of politeness, is crisscrossed by all sorts of actual differences of status, and furthermore, by a general feeling which hardly exists in the United States, that some sort of status, even family status involving heredity, is in the order of nature. I am aware that I have produced a paradox, after warning against the dangers of paradox. But this means merely that I am puzzled about the matter. Somehow the Frenchman comes closer in ordinary life than the rest of us Westerners to accepting with that kind of incomplete resignation we call irony the fact that the ideal is not the real. Even in the service industries—hotels, restaurants, domestic services, the travel industry—which put egalitarian ideals to one of their hardest tests, Frenchmen seem proud of doing a good job. This pride, which quite without ironic overtones used also to be evident in corresponding stations in life in England, I think does show signs of diminishing there.

But we are getting beyond our depths in social psychology. There is, I think, some relation between this French willingness to accept the limitation of this world and that very important fact of French life I have already brought up— French addiction to the small enterprise, the small farm, the family business, their reluctance, in spite of striking exceptions in steel and in a few other industries, to go all out for large-scale industry after the model set by the United States, Germany, Britain, and Russia. At any rate, this addiction to smallness, to "individualism" if you like, is one of the things that endures in France, so much so that the Communists there have had to pretend in their propaganda that Communism is designed especially to protect the peasant-proprietor and the small shopkeeper.

The Survival of Individualism

The fact is that a good deal of what American liberals scornfully, and American businessmen praisefully, call "rugged individualism" persists all over Western Europe even in these days of the welfare state. I propose to take up in conclusion some examples of this survival in business and in intellectual life.

There is little doubt that it is more difficult for the born entrepreneur to get a start in the modern West than it used to be. Yet even in our own day Mr. Howard Johnson has had a Horatio Alger career, starting on a shoestring with a neighborhood icecream business in suburban Boston. The British analogue to Mr. Johnson is a man named Butlin, who from modest beginnings has built up a chain of holiday camps which are—I hope—the last word in mass catering. There seems to be everything—except the possibility of a quiet life—in these Butlin camps. The vacationer gets a standard, uniformly priced package of delights, all provided automatically. A Butlin resort must indeed seem to the sensitive intellectual evidence that perhaps the George Orwell who wrote *1984* was after all a realist, but the point I wish to make is that these halls of regimented pleasure are no product of government planning, but of private business initiative.

Indeed, the Europeans are by no means as far behind us in providing new material comforts for the unvanished middle classes as we often think they are. The Hôtel du Rhone in Geneva, opened in 1951, by no means a hotel de luxe, but aimed rather at the kind of clientele our Statler hotels are aimed at, is a model of unobtrusive modernity, from its ventilation system to its synthetic floor covering, a kind of superlinoleum on which one almost floats. During the last war a colleague and I were able to rent in London a small house which not only had an electric refrigerator and a silex coffeepot, but a central heating system that really worked. We couldn't of course boost the living room up to American standards, which I take to be about blood-heat, but we could get it up almost to 70 degrees Fahrenheit. Though I may be overdoing the role of children in contemporary France, I cannot resist bringing up here the *salon de l'enfance* held yearly in the Grand Palais in Paris. This exhibition is a triumph of ingenuity in the business of providing amusement and perhaps also instruction for the child. There are all sorts of toys and gadgets, all sorts of plans for a better childhood. Even American children would find something new there.

In another field there is the postwar blossoming of the Italian moving-picture industry. A benevolent government has no doubt helped that blossoming, but on the whole it has been the work of private initiative, and I think I am justified in taking over the approved Hollywood term, "industry." Perhaps, like other periods of successful effort in any art, this flowering has come about chiefly through the presence of a few gifted individuals. We are still so ignorant of all that makes for such a flowering that we may be justified in calling the coming-together of such gifted individuals "accidental." Still, we must suspect that there are some social factors behind this sort of achievement. My point is that from war-torn and poverty-stricken Italy there have come better motion pictures—and incidentally better novels —than from the apparently prosperous Italy of Mussolini.

One could cite many more evidences of the continued ability of Western Europeans to produce something new, to create. The recent rise of the West German economy, which I have not witnessed at first hand, is a clear example of the persistence in the mixed economy of those factors of individual inventiveness and enterprise which we are often told were extinguished as early as 1914. But I must pass on to matters more purely of the spirit.

It is very difficult to analyze the temper of one's own time, especially with respect to those signs of decay and death which preoccupy a Spengler, a Sorokin, or a Toynbee. A Roman prophet of doom like Tacitus, we now see, was in part right. But the difficulty is that there are always prophets of doom. It is worth saying again: optimism and pessimism among intellectuals and the intellectual classes are not chemical elements, and they cannot be readily measured. Anyone with an elementary training in historical research and a good library at his disposal could put together, starting with Plato and the Hebrew prophets, an almost continuous chain of quotations like those from Lewis Mumford, T. S. Eliot, and Katherine Anne Porter with which I began this study. There might be occasional gaps during the period of the so-called Dark Ages, for lack of surviving records, but by and large it is true that in every Western generation some articulate person has announced that his is the worst of possible worlds, that his society is sick unto death. The specific details of their complaints do indeed vary, as do their remedies—for, though some of our modern philosophers of history rather gloss over this fact, almost all of them do have remedies to propose, cherish carefully some hopes even for this lost world.

Yet very few of us can see history as a dead-level of unchanging reality beneath a mere froth of change, or else a mere tidal ebb and flow. Something which, with the proviso that we are using a certain kind of metaphor, I am willing to call death, happened to Periclean Athens. All I really wish to maintain now is that kind of death has not yet happened to Western Europe, and that there are no unmistakable signs that kind of death is about to happen there. Something is happening, which may be no more than a change of life; and it is happening very slowly, as it must in that ill-understood organism—again a metaphor—we call society. The old Europe is still alive, and nowhere more clearly than in that great variety of ideas about the meaning of life I have called its multanimity.

Some years ago I was talking over his thesis subject with Mr. Alan Brown, now president of Hobart and William Smith Colleges. The thesis, since published, dealt with the Metaphysical Society, an informal group of distinguished mid-Victorians which met for dinner and high discussion. We were discussing its very broad membership, how it numbered Roman Catholics like Manning and Ward, Anglicans like Thirlwall and Gladstone, Unitarians like Martineau, Comtian positivists like Frederic Harrison, agnostics like T. H. Huxley, indeed a whole spectrum of English attitudes toward the ultimates. All these men met together in friendliness and outspoken frankness over a good dinner in a famous London restaurant. At one point Mr. Brown remarked parenthetically, "Of course, you can't imagine anything like that today." He was indeed right in the main. There is a bitterness in our contemporary intellectual differences, perhaps also a desire for publicity, which works against so quiet a gathering. We are not all of us quite so sure as were the Victorians that metaphysics is worth all that trouble. These and many many other factors, of great concern to the intellectual historian, militate against just such a society today, even in England, where high debate still rules in common room and—somewhat muted and mixed with less high matters—also over the air-waves of the British Broadcasting Corporation.

Yet I am sure Mr. Brown did not mean that the great debate does not go on in our way by other means, and with almost as much range and freedom. For it certainly does so continue, heightened by the fact that many of its participants, now as then, engage in it with the fond hope that some day soon it will end in agreement as all men embrace the true faith. We know that the debate goes on here in America, even though Lord Russell and other interested persons tell the world that no one in the United States dares say what he thinks, unless he agrees with, say, Senator Taft —or was it Senator McCarthy? Americans—and incidentally, Frenchmen in modern times—appear always to have lacked the equanimity that made the British Metaphysical Society possible. Nowhere in the West, however, is the debate silenced, and nowhere does it seem yet to be the kind of struggle in which the political victors are determined to silence their opponents in death. In Russia, the debate was just such a deadly struggle, which is in part why it has ended there, for the time at least. In Western Europe it is very much alive. There are indeed totalitarians of both Right and Left in Europe who would end it, totalitarians who enjoy the paradoxical freedom we believers in the endless debate seem bound by our very belief to give them. There are unquestionably such believers in totalitarian solutions in the United States. But they have not won the day in Western Europe, nor here, and I do not think they are winning it. Our *habits* of actual diversity of opinion on high matters and low are perhaps even stronger than our *faith* in its theoretical desirability, which is surely one reason why the heart of the West, Western Europe, most of the Americas, most of Western society overseas elsewhere have not gone totalitarian. Habit is a more important ally of ours than the rationalist liberal likes to admit. Nowhere in Western Europe is habit yet on the side of the totalitarian state and society.

Here I may risk making a proposition perhaps dangerously optimistic. I think it possible that even were the Gaullist Right or the Communist Left to gain control in France, even were English socialists to try to realize the thinly disguised enlightened despotism always threatening in England from Bentham through the old Fabians to the new—even in these unlikely cases I suspect some freedom of speech, some diversity, some of the old Adam as centuries of multanimity in Europe have shaped him would survive, and would eventually wreck the attempt at totalitarian control. You may remember how during the war and the Vichy regime in France many Frenchmen insisted that the new model France had to have the proper one-party organization. The difficulty was that there were so many of these *partis uniques*—at least three major ones and a number of minor ones.

To the quality of this intellectual life in Western Europe I shall return in my last chapter. It may be degenerate, and may deserve those ingenious and often searching epithets Mr. Arnold Toynbee has drawn from his vast knowledge of Greco-Roman culture—schism in the soul, archaism, futurism, pammixia, and proletarianization. Again I call attention to the difficulty that at once arises if you take high culture, and particularly the arts, as measures of the age and health of a society. A list parellel to the list I suggested of

thinkers sure that their own period was hopelessly degenerate could be drawn up, certainly for the last few centuries, numbering critics sure that the then modern art
meant the end of the road, a dissolution of all the decencies
and the beauties. An English critic about 1810 remarked
that Beethoven might fool his own countrymen, but that
Englishmen knew him for a charlatan. My own favorite is
the Boston legend that when Symphony Hall was built in
1904 a conservative outraged by modernism suggested that
instead of "exit" there be inscribed "this way out in case
of—Brahms!"

All I wish to establish now is the fact that the old variety
of views and tastes still obtains in Western Europe. The
academicians still struggle with the *avant-garde*. Heartbreak
House—its heart actually I think in rather better shape than
it used to be in the old Bloomsbury days—still looks scornfully and wistfully toward a Horseback Hall no longer in
its best days, but still riding to the hounds. Positivism,
materialism, secularism, and all their variants, after having
been buried by their profounder enemies in a suitably shal-
low grave, turn out to be quite alive. Christianity, which
the positivists had buried a bit earlier, has of course persisted, and indeed gained as it usually does at the end of a
great war.

I shall not attempt here a survey of the richness of contemporary cultural life in Western Europe. Even Mr.
Shirer, however, somewhat existentially seeks to rally his
reader by remarking of *Midcentury Journey*, "If you come
along with me on this midcentury journey, you will feel
proud and glad, I think, as I did, despite the tribulations
which beset us all, to be living at this tumultuous time in
so great an age." This may not be a true *Blütezeit*, a high

point in cultural history. But if Europe really is sunk in
decay, it is certainly not a somnolent decay. I would not
question Mr. T. S. Eliot's high place in the line of prophets
and witnesses that begins with Plato. Perhaps the world
will end, as he says in lines now safely in the anthologies,
"not with a bang but a whimper." To me at least it looks
as if contemporary Europe were indulging in many more
bangs than whimpers—making, in fact, so much noise that
one is reminded rather of a nursery than of a death ward.

IV

The Possible Future

European Union

I have in the last two chapters insisted that Western Europe today is, in spite of the horrors of our time, as a whole materially richer than ever before; this is a verifiable fact of the external world, even if we verify through statistics. I have also maintained that one who knew Europe thirty years ago will quite readily recognize Europe today, that the past of Europe is in part also its present. This statement too is reasonably verifiable. Finally, I have said that Europe seems to me alive rather than dead, even in a sense youthful rather than senile. That is of course a private judgment.

I come in this last chapter to a set of problems where no man's answers can be more than guesses. I shall write about the possible future of Western Europe, and shall emphasize the new rather than the old. But I trust I shall be building on the firm ground of the old, the known, the established.

The most important new thing in Western Europe would be some greater actual union, some effective political, or at least economic, integration of the whole or part of the region. Now the voluntary successful union in a common state, a common government, of any contemporary European countries would be a revolution more striking than any of the innumerable revolutions of morals, taste, politics, and science our publicists have noted, or perhaps imagined, in the last few decades. No such voluntary union has taken place there since the mid-nineteenth century unification of Italy and Germany—and to many historians those national unifications seem more forced than voluntary. We Americans must be especially careful not to let our hopes simplify our thinking about European political unity, and especially not to let that simplification take this form, so irritating to Europeans: we Americans got together in the eighteenth century, so you people ought to be able to get together now.

Several kinds of functional coöperative undertakings among the states of Western Europe seem to me to be among the possible futures of the region. No political union, no federal union to produce a *Bundesstaat*, or true federal state, seems to me to be among the possible futures. Here indeed I assume a future of a generation or so, a future which for many of us will someday be a present. What Europe will be like a century or two from now, or a millennium from now, is a perfectly legitimate subject for speculation, but it is not one that concerns me now. The human beings, leaders and led, who would in our days have to make and carry out the decisions to create a West European state are in my opinion quite unable to make and carry out these decisions. Their past performances—and history can be at least a kind of form-sheet—show that they cannot go much faster than they are now going. Full European union, or even such a union as that of Belgium, Netherlands, and Luxembourg into a single new state, would be like asking a top-notch miler today to cut thirty seconds or so off his time, which is impossible. Note that I use a human runner, not a motorcar or an airplane, as my example. Men are not machines, even if advanced eighteenth-century thinkers like La Mettrie thought them so. Darwinism here reinforces Christianity on one important point: man is not perfectible within the time-scale of human technology.

I realize very well that on this as on so many problems people's minds tend to be made up—as mine clearly is—and that facts, statistics, and metaphors no matter how skillfully marshaled will not change our minds for many of us. The European federationist can get quite different results from my own figure of speech. The miler, he would say, doesn't need to make any such fantastic advance as cutting thirty seconds off his time: all he needs to do is set a new record for himself; and for that all he needs is the best track the experts can build, and the will and the heart to go after the record. The most hopeful federationist might push aside as irrelevant all my figure of speech except that of speed and say: we aren't dealing with unaided human muscles, but with man's amazing ability to use his brains to get beyond his muscles; national sovereignty and the United Nations are horse-and-buggy; we've got the fine internal combustion engine of World Government right at hand; all we have to do is crank it up, and off we go.

I probably haven't done very well in my attempt to see the other fellow's point of view. The World Federationists, even the European Unionists, will feel that I have caricatured them. So we had better leave the matter here, and proceed to a much more concrete matter, the actual ways in which Europeans *are* trying to work together, the ways in which they are actually getting beyond the sovereign nation-state in practice. The sum total of these ways is impressive, quite enough to persuade me that the most likely future for Western Europe lies in the attempt to make existing methods of coöperation more effective, and in exploring the possibility of adding new ways.

First of all, almost all of the Western European nations are part of the United Nations. Now to a historian the United Nations seem to be in pretty direct succession to the League of Nations of 1919, the Congress System of 1815, and the Concert of Europe of the early eighteenth century, to go no further back. The pessimist may say these attempts to organize peace, occurring as they do after particularly severe general or world wars, are no more than the drunkard's morning-after repentance and of no more lasting significance. The optimist may say that these attempts to organize peace are the conscious efforts of the sounder parts of society to rally the recuperative forces of men in society after the disasters of war, and that on the whole they show over the centuries a slow but appreciable progress. I find myself agreeing with the optimist, who is surely no very wild one if he finds the United Nations of 1953 an improvement over the alliance system of the early eighteenth century. The United Nations may be basically no more than a gathering of diplomatists, and it certainly is not a government, not a superstate. But it is an elaborately organized set of institutions, staffed by trained specialists, and at the very least it channels disputes, provides possibilities of settlement. It has obviously and almost miraculously to some of us what the League of Nations had not, the wholehearted participation of the American government and of the majority of the American people.

Then there is the so-called Schuman Plan, which has now begun operations. Six West European countries, France, the three countries of Benelux, West Germany, and Italy, have actually undertaken to set up a joint authority which has constitutional power to make and enforce laws binding on all six countries. Its power is limited to two closely related industries, iron and coal, together with the materials and equipment necessary to make steel. But it is fair to say that in respect to one specific field of government activity, these six countries have agreed to give up part of their "sovereignty." In a limited field, the new coal and steel authority really seems to be supranational, to be a *Bundesstaat* or true federal state, not just a *Staatenbund*, or league of states. The authority, on paper at least, really has authority. It remains to see whether the plan will work. Its governing body is almost certain to make sooner or later a decision so unpalatable to one of the member states that the government of that state will refuse to accept the decision. We must not set too high our hopes for this pioneering attempt to get beyond the nation-state. Given reasonably stable world economic conditions, it has I think a chance of getting consolidated enough to stand the strains it will have to face. A depression, or even a serious recession, may quite possibly wreck it before it has a chance to establish itself as a going concern. But the mere fact that the Schuman Plan is being given a trial shows that West Europe has not lost the ability to make—and make by agreement arrived at by discussion—a major political experiment. This does look like something other than a patient turning over in his sickbed.

NATO, the North Atlantic Treaty Organization, is another experiment in international organization for regular, disciplined action, not merely for consultation and coöperation. The historian is bound to see in this organization basically a military coalition of the kind that has always come into being when the balance of power in our state-system is as sharply defined as it is by the present rivalry between the United States and Russia. But it is already, and if plans for a European army work out it will be even more, a much tighter military coalition than we have ever had at comparable periods in the history of our Western state-system, which is now in fact a world-system. This is a danger, but it is also a promise. There is in the development of international military organization the same tendency to a closer and more efficient working together—still well short of perfect communion—we have noted in diplomatic organization. NATO, like the United Nations, is at least a better piece of machinery than its forerunners of the eighteenth century, better than earlier models. I have always cherished the story, which like most such stories is very hard to establish as true, that in the first campaigns against revolutionary France in 1792 the allied armies of Prussia and Austria were so mutually distrustful that they commonly set out sentries each against the other as well as against the French. In the war of 1914–1918 a unified high command was not achieved on the Western front until the last moment, and there was never a single Allied army. In this last war we and the British achieved an extraordinary interleaving of staffs not only in planning but in the field. There were difficulties, but they were overcome, sometimes in the way indicated by one of the folk stories about General Eisenhower. The general is said to have relieved an American officer of his command, not because the officer called his British subordinate a son-of-a-bitch, but because he called him a *British* son-of-a-bitch. In NATO we are trying to pick up where we left off at the end of the war, and not altogether without success. We should not be too impatient with the French if they slow up, or even prevent, the achievement of a fully integrated European army. A NATO army even with separable national units that hung together as well as did Eisenhower's in 1944 would in itself be a remarkable achievement.

There is also the Council of Europe, which unlike the Schuman Plan Organization, NATO, and indeed some of the functional carry-overs from the League of Nations, is so far an affair of words rather than deeds. The Council of Europe was founded on May 5, 1949. Its foundation members were Belgium, Denmark, France, Ireland, Italy, Luxembourg, the Netherlands, Norway, Sweden, and the United Kingdom. Western Germany and the Saar became associate members, with right of representation in the Consultative Assembly only, in 1950. The seat of the Council is at Strasbourg in Alsace. It is not by any means a wholly unofficial pressure group of propagandists and planners, like the numerous groups organized throughout the West for Union Now, World Federation, and the like. The Council itself is composed of the Foreign Ministers of the member states. The Consultative Assembly, delegates to which are appointed as each member state wishes, is for the most part composed of deputies from the respective parliamentary bodies. There is a professional secretariat. The debates in the Assembly are public, and are reported in the major newspapers.

The Council has announced that its work is supplementary to, and in no sense an undermining of, the work of the United Nations and other established international bodies. It is certainly, in the minds of such influential sponsors as Sir Winston Churchill and M. Paul Reynaud, a preliminary to a real European union. One of the best brief accounts of its work is the final chapter of M. Paul Reynaud's *Unite or*

Perish, published in English in New York in 1951. A plan for a closer political union of the six nations of the Schuman Plan—France, West Germany, Italy, the Netherlands, Belgium, and Luxembourg—has recently been passed unanimously at Strasbourg. It has not at this writing in midsummer of 1953 become a reality, and it may not for some time. Britain, at least, is apparently somewhat more benevolent toward the Council than toward the Schuman Plan.

It would be premature to hail in Strasbourg the European equivalent of our Philadelphia Convention of 1787, from which emerged the present Constitution of the United States of America. A United States of Europe—even of Western, democratic Europe—will be very hard indeed to found. But they are making a conscious beginning of the task at Strasbourg. Men actually engaged responsibly in the work of governing their own countries—politicians, if the word doesn't offend you—are at work in the Council of Europe, and not merely publicists, political scientists, propagandists. Experience suggests that if the job is to be done, politicians have to do it. There were politicians at work in Philadelphia in 1787.

Finally, there is the Saar. Last July the German Bundestag firmly announced that the Saar must be part of Germany. The French, apparently, would be content with an autonomous Saarland, even a "Europeanized" Saarland, tied economically to France. No sensible commentator would risk a firm prognosis here. The Saar may prove to be the specific case that keeps Germany and France divided; or it may be the specific case on which hinges the whole process of reconciliation between these old enemies. This tiny but rich coal region, highly industrialized, and German by language and tradition, is a fascinating test case. For if the

Saar is, quite literally, German at heart, its economic interests as the world now is lie very clearly in free trade with France. Rarely are emotions and interests, heart and head, so neatly opposed in this world. We should at least learn something about the relative importance of these contrary pulls on a human group from what happens in the Saar in the near future. Much more hopeful we cannot be. Heaven on earth is not likely to start in the Saar.

I wrote earlier that our American success in getting beyond the little red one-room schoolhouse to the graded district school might throw light on the problem of greater union among West European states. We Americans have reformed the rural school system; we have not reformed the whole system of rural local government. In a democracy, those reforms get through behind which there are concrete interests and enthusiasms as well as abstract ideas and ideals. I realize I am making a hasty generalization, begging, in a way, a question which is at the heart of social psychology. Perhaps I had better rest with my concrete comparisons. The Schuman Plan, and some of the functional organizations of the United Nations, seem to me like the district school plan, practical; total union for all Western Europe in our time seems to me like a plan for total reform of our local government—or better yet, like Mr. W. Y. Elliott's ingenious plan for cutting down the number of our forty-eight—or forty-nine—states, impractical.

I have hitherto been working on the evident, if unstated, assumption that for the kind of world most of us Americans want some stronger union of Western Europe is desirable as a long-term aim. I do indeed think that such a union would help make the kind of world we want. But a historian

addicted to the Machiavellian view, to what is often called realism, would have to warn that a Europe—even the truncated Europe we have been calling "Western Europe"— might, if by some miracle it could be forged into a really united state, turn out to be a rival, even an enemy. Such a state, especially if by retaining some at least of the overseas possessions of existing states like Britain, France, and Belgium it had access to important raw materials, would be as much a superpower as the United States or the USSR. It would have a greater population than either, and an industrial potential quite as great. No such state seems to me possible in our own time, but the remote possibility that it might arise should not in the least deter us from trying to help the formation of a West European union.

In our Western state-system those states in the past which have attained the kind of leadership or hegemony we Americans now have, seem always to have pursued a policy of "divide and rule." This is certainly true even of one of the best of them, Victorian England. "Divide and rule" is an easy, in a sense a natural, policy, a policy which has been at the root of the balance-of-power principle. It has helped to preserve our system of nation-states from imperial domination, helped to preserve a concrete territorial and material basis for the spiritual good as well as for the bad in what we call nationalism; but it has also prevented any federal union transcending that system and its major evil, war. I think we have got to gamble on a possible union of Europe as a step in transcending the politics of balance of power, as a step to a distant but not impossible world government based on the federal, not the imperialist, principle, on consent, not on force.

The Economic Future

I come now to the possible economic future of Western Europe. I have already stated the basic economic problem that confronts the area: how to support in the style to which they have become accustomed and which they will not willingly abandon, some fifty, perhaps a hundred, millions of people for whom food and other basic raw materials do not exist within the area, and cannot by existing means be produced there. We are concerned with the reasonable future of a generation or two. It is perhaps conceivable that the chemists, who have already done wonders, will do something really astounding, such as making cellulose digestible for human beings. Even then, I expect that many Englishmen would insist that the oaks of England were not designed for eating. Seriously, though scientific agriculture, technology, and good administration can add something to the food and other raw material resources of Western Europe, though new sources of power in the region may be found, it is clear that Western Europe will have to live in the immediate future as it has lived in the past few centuries, by exchanging finished goods and services for food and other raw materials.

This means that somewhere else on earth people will have to send food and raw materials to Western Europe and accept finished goods and services in return; or, to drive home the obvious, it means that somewhere outside of Europe there must be areas which are not economically autarkic, which produce more food, oil, rubber, metals and other raw materials than they need, and less machinery, textiles, ships, other finished goods, banking and insurance than they need. Now, once more talking about a measurable future, not a far-distant one, I think we can find right within our own borders evidence that within a given great free-trading area, an old industrial region far more deprived than even Western Europe of food and raw materials can do very well for itself. There is the story, unquestionably Californian in origin, about the Californian who remarked that if the United States had been settled in the opposite direction, from the Pacific Coast instead of from the Atlantic, New England would still be a howling wilderness. But the country was settled from the Atlantic side. New England, shut off completely from the rest of the world, would starve even more quickly than would Old England so shut off. And indeed the prophets of doom have been killing off New England for at least a century. But, though New England is not booming like Texas, Yankees are very far from starving. Iowa farmers still buy New England cotton goods, even though they buy more cotton goods from the Piedmont, and they buy Yankee household appliances; and Yankees still enjoy Iowa corn-fed pork.

Of course if Iowa and other parts of the country could build trade barriers against New England, if each American region could and did try to be self-sufficient, we in New England could not carry on as we are doing. Within a free-trading area the classical economic doctrine of comparative advantage still holds. If there were, not the absolute free trade Cobden and his fellows preached, but some approximation to free trade over large parts of the world, then I think it obvious that Old England, for example, could hold its own at least as well as New England has. It is still cheaper to produce knives in Sheffield than in Australia, and cheaper to produce mutton in Australia than in Yorkshire.

There is, even in our neo-mercantilist world, enough of
the old sort of international trade so that, with some help
from us in the form of what are really subsidies, Western
Europe has been able to keep going, as we have seen, on a
relatively high standard of living. If America can convert
those subsidies to trade, if, to be concrete, we can abstain
from developing all our industrial capacities for the sake
of a world balance, then Europe will be well on the way to
recovery. Even more important would be the lifting of
trade restrictions within the British Commonwealth and
the French Union, in South America, and elsewhere. The
experts are working toward this goal, and though it is a
goal which public opinion finds it hard to get excited about
—economics will probably never quite live down that tag,
the "dismal science"—it is surely a goal of major importance,
and one toward which American energies should be directed.

In the short term, at least, I think we should soften as
much as we can our intransigeant attitude toward what is
left of European colonialism. Even on idealistic grounds, it
seems clear that the too rapid emancipation of regions like
Central Africa, Madagascar, Malaya is no kindness to native
populations. The topic is one on which, like many we have
touched upon here, emotional balance is hard to attain. The
metaphor of "middle of the road" may be given a twist that
makes it most unsatisfactory. It is not, in the presence of
traffic, a good place to drive. Yet on this specific problem,
few indeed would really sympathize with Robespierre's
famous outburst, when in debate it was brought out that
the French sugar islands in the Caribbean were peopled
largely by blacks not ready for the practice of Liberty,
Equality, Fraternity, that immediate wholesale emancipa-

tion of the blacks would be disastrous. No matter, cried Robespierre, "let the colonies perish rather than a principle!"

Now if the English got out of Malaya, the French out of Indo-China, if all the European countries got out of Africa, the consequences would probably not be just what they were when the French got out of—were driven out of—Haiti. You may even argue that it was better for the Haitians to undergo the tragic history that has been theirs since 1789 as free men than to have been nursed along even by a benevolent France. Yet in no very good sense were they free men under Christophe or Dessalines, or under the corrupt rule of their nineteenth-century presidents. We nursed the Filipinos for half a century before we cut them loose—and even so, they must have our "protection" for some time to come.

The British and the French in their different ways are both trying to preserve some degree of tutelage over their black and brown dependents. It is a hard task for them to alter the past of exploitation. The very sore spot of Kenya points up the difficulty, for in Kenya the whites have the best lands, and the blacks, who are multiplying under conditions of public law and public health at least far better than in the past, have not enough land for themselves. Perhaps the Mau Mau, like the blacks in Haiti, should be allowed to drive out the white landowners. But again, a Kenyan Christophe—no unlikely thing—is not a prospect even the "liberal" should contemplate happily.

Actually no one region like Kenya is wholly typical. The whites never have become farmers or grazers in the lowlands of tropical Africa. Tribal organization may there be modernized into effective modern self-government. The whole Near East, including French North Africa, is far too advanced already in nationalism, and in a rudimentary way in economic life, for sheer nursing along by Europeans. Malaya presents the special problem of a large and not yet assimilated Chinese minority. And so it goes throughout the old colonial world.

We can but urge patience and an experimental attitude. The spirit of Robespierre must not be ours. Reactionary elements in Britain and in France certainly would like to go back simply to their own good old days, but they are not in power and it is fairly safe to say that in both these great colonial powers men of good will are struggling with the problems the past has saddled them with. One may hope that the precedent of India, Pakistan, and Ceylon, free nations but not wholly cut off politically from their former "masters," can be gradually extended, and that the colored peoples of Africa and southeast Asia will not have to undergo the fate of Haiti.

There is, moreover, a factor present today that was not present in Haiti in the nineteenth century. We have come to realize that when Western Europeans step out of Asiatic "colonial" areas, Eastern Europeans—Russians—step in, directly or through their native stooges. We have even apparently decided for the present to support wicked France in her colony of Indo-China. But even were Russian pressure somewhat relieved, I do not think we should urge on Western Europe a too hasty abandonment of what is left of the colonial system. We must not forget the upperdog in concern for the underdog. In this imperfect world, some temporary maintenance of this system may well make the difference between the survival of a strong and prosperous Western Europe and its dangerous economic weakening.

And economic weakening of Western Europe is almost certain to lead to grave political disturbances there. Europe is still the place where the big wars, the bad wars, start.

If Western Europe's economic future depends in part on the maintenance of an exchange of European manufactured goods and services for overseas food and raw materials, it depends in the longer run on the maintenance of Western Europe's comparative advantage—that is, on the region's ability to produce for export goods which overseas regions will prefer to what they might produce themselves. There are many economic measures of this kind of advantage—measures of cost and productivity; I have deliberately put the matter in terms of overseas demand for European goods, if only to remind you that the ultimate consumers count.

For those who believe that the kind of industrial productivity needed to maintain Western Europe's export markets is directly measured by the closeness with which a given society approaches standards set by Herbert Spencer's *Social Statics* and *The Man vs. the State*, Western Europe is pretty far gone on the road to extinction. These believers in dogmatic laissez faire are by no means limited to the United States. There are Englishmen who hold that theirs is an ill-fare not a welfare state, Frenchmen who think their government far-gone in socialism. But we must not allow ourselves to get involved in the general problem of whether the increasing use of government intervention to achieve higher incomes for the poorer classes is the road to serfdom and ruin. Such use of government, whether or not you label it socialism, collectivism, the welfare state, or even New Deal or Fair Deal, has been universal in the West, though varying greatly in different countries. I think that on the whole the account I have already given shows that such use of government intervention in Western Europe has not prevented a very high degree of economic recovery in the years since the war. For the immediate future, if we give up oversimple and overabstract debates as to the virtues and vices of socialism or individualism and concentrate on what seems likely to happen in Western Europe, we shall conclude that there are good chances of economic survival.

There is no chance that anywhere in Western Europe men will go back to Herbert Spencer, to formulas like "that government governs best which governs least, and least expensively." Social-security measures of many kinds, government ownership and operation of railways and some major heavy industries, price controls and regulation of all sorts will be the rule not only in England and Sweden, but to a degree in all Western Europe. But, unless all signs fail, this will not mean an extinction of human ability to invent, to improve, to work effectively. It will not mean a dead level of stagnation, if only because the kind of collectivism that has grown up in the modern Western world has not in fact turned out to be the simple bureaucratic formula nineteenth-century critics of collectivist ideas thought "socialism" in practice would be.

One of the actual forms the economic development of Europe is increasingly taking is that of the public corporation, a form which already has many variants in different countries. The public corporation is in part at least the result of an effort by its planners to avoid the evils so often predicted of socialism—bureaucratic methods, subordination to the whims of politics, lack of team spirit, lack of initiative. The public corporation is a genuine corporation in something like the old medieval sense; that is, it is a corporate group with a life of its own, a sphere of action, an independence based on rights—the rights set up in its charter. Whether it can in a pinch maintain those rights against a government will no doubt be decisively tested somewhere before long. Certainly the rights of the public corporation are not unlimited, in Great Britain, for instance. They are certainly less than, by the precedent of the Dartmouth College case and much more constitutional law, we assume in America are the rights of any private corporation. But they are not inexistent; these public corporations are not just the creatures of the government.

On the whole the history of one of the best known of these corporations shows that they can indeed have a life, a spirit of their own. The British Broadcasting Corporation has often been reproached with excessive timidity, with a desire not to offend politicians, with self-righteously seeking to improve public tastes, and with also catering to the low tastes of the public. In short, radio in Britain, where it is in the hands of a public corporation, and radio in the United States, where it is in the hands of a few private corporations, seems to arouse much the same sort of reactions among the people of the two countries. I do not wish to deny that there are differences between the radio fare in the two countries, but, even though in Britain you do not have the advertising dinned in your ear, I am much more struck with the similarities. I grant you that in this country individuals have made money out of the actual process of broadcasting and that in England they have not, although the BBC is of course not a drain on the Exchequer. Moreover, it is sometimes forgotten that in Britain the actual manufacture of radio and television equipment is in private hands, a good deal of it in the hands of a great international corporation, that of Phillips. But it is surely striking that in both the

United States and in Britain the last thirty years have seen the successful rise to a prominent place in the economy of a great new industry of radio and television.

British nationalization has in general taken a form that may be described rather as a public corporation than as a simple government "department," like the Post Office. Coal mining, and indeed the distribution of coal, is now a monopoly, a nationalized industry. It has, incidentally, to face the competition of oil and electricity, so it is not quite the monopoly that horrified some classical economists. The management is unified in a central board, but the actual administration is broken down by regions which have at least the autonomy of any organized group in real life. For in real life the absolutely perfect chain of command, the push-button organization, simply does not exist. Management and labor are still true groups; there are still unions, and as a matter of fact, still strikes in the British coal industry. The managers are indeed no longer responsible to stockholders, but it is a commonplace nowadays that they are not so responsible in any immediate sense in capitalist societies. The managers of the British coal industry are indeed responsible to the government, are appointed by the government. But the fact is that they are still essentially recruited by and among themselves; they are not politicians. We need not go all the way with Mr. James Burnham's *Managerial Revolution* to recognize that the modern corporation, in the United States as in Britain, is no longer the simple one-man affair of the classical entrepreneur. The coal industry in Britain is a vast corporation, free indeed from the pressure to make a profit for stockholders, but otherwise facing the necessity—including the necessity of meeting competition of other corporations offering other fuels to the consumer—of producing and marketing its product efficiently. It starts with serious handicaps—an obsolescent plant, a lack of an abundant, easily worked supply of coal, and a past of bad labor relations. It has not worked the miracles some British socialists hoped for and expected, but it has not failed dismally as some conservatives were sure it would fail. It has, in short, proved to be a corporation with a life of its own.

Americans, save for the economic die-hards, have indeed been better disposed toward our own best-known example of the public corporation. The TVA has had an amazingly good press, both here and abroad. Europeans who come to this country are most eager to see this specimen of American enterprise in a new form. Yet TVA would have shocked Herbert Spencer—and not only Herbert Spencer. It has, however, clearly kept itself free from the kind of politics the older economists were sure would lame any experiment of the sort. It has not been free of public opinion, has indeed done a very good and very modern job in public relations. One may hope that we can be at least as patient with European attempts to do something of the sort as we have been with the TVA.

Indeed, in this whole matter of modern economic organization the basic problems—how to reconcile size with efficiency, how to reconcile growth and innovation with stability, how to reconcile reward, incentive, indeed at bottom private property, with a high minimal standard of living for everyone—are problems which in the free West we are trying to solve by the methods summed up in the phrase a "mixed economy" and not by the methods of Russian

Communism. This is a common effort, in which we should regard ourselves rather as partners of Western Europe than as rivals, if only because if Europe fails to make a mixed economy work she will be forced to try a communist economy, with disastrous results for us. There is no chance whatever that Western Europe will return to laissez faire. I think, however, that the record of the postwar years shows that barring an immediate general war, Western Europe is on its way to make its mixed economy work.

One of the interesting questions that faces the economist is that of measuring the exact degree of the mixture in a given mixed economy. For one thing, if you seek for a statistical measure of the "free" sector of the economy as distinguished from the "nationalized" or "collectivized" sector, you run up against the fact that there are many degrees of nationalization, from the public corporation like the BBC or that curious French hybrid, the *Régie Renault* which administers the great Renault motor works, taken over at the end of the war because the management had collaborated so completely with the Germans, right down to the Post Office, which is, I take it, a completely "socialistic" institution even in the United States. Moreover, the free sector of the economy is everywhere subject to various forms of government regulation and especially to government fiscal policy. Finally, the present high level of military expenditures takes from all Western nations a large slice of the national income. Omitting these military expenditures it does seem likely that even in the British economy private industry, including of course agriculture, accounts for the lion's share of the gross national product, probably indeed well over sixty per cent, or more. That does not seem to me a danger point.

The Spirit of Western Europe

I come now to the central problem of this book: is the state of mind of the peoples of Western Europe, their "temper," such that they can face with energy and confidence the task of rebuilding, which is really a task of building anew? Or are they really—I get back to the inescapable metaphor with which I began—*old* peoples, unable to make new responses, worn-out mentally and physically, in short, finished, done for. A great many Americans, certainly, make the offhand assumption that Western Europe is finished. I am shocked to find that many of our undergraduates not only think of France as a negligible factor in world affairs, but are not even aware that France has ever been a leader of civilization. As for Britain, they think of her with a certain degree of *Schadenfreude* as almost wholly dependent on our bounty.

Alluring though the temptation to try to analyze the state of the West in Spenglerian or Toynbean terms may be, I think we must put the temptation behind us. As I have perhaps insisted too much already, we just cannot make the diagnosis of senility or decay in a contemporary society. We cannot even say that if everybody in a given society were in the state of mind of the writers I quoted at the beginning of this book, then that society really is on its last legs. For such a statement would be an absurdity, quite contrary to any possibility, if only because no society is composed solely of intellectuals. It might be less absurd to say that if everybody, or at least the great majority of a society showed by their actual behavior that they despaired utterly of life on this earth, that they had no future, then that society could not exist. But this supposition is as absurd as the first, and makes no sense empirically, not even for that classic example of death-and-decay, the only one in our society we know much about, the break-up of the Roman Empire in the West. For it was the toughness of the millions of people of that Empire, the common people even more than the intellectuals, that enabled them eventually to absorb the German barbarians, and survive. If they had not had that toughness, I should not have been able just now to write "survive," but would have had to write something like "ueberleben."

But I am getting drawn in spite of myself into the vortex of the philosophy of history. That the peoples of Western Europe are not sunk in an almost unthinkable supineness is clear from their re-action—that well-worn tag is really apt, for they did *act*—to Hitler. What the British did we all know; but we all too commonly blame the continental peoples, and especially the French, Belgians, and Dutch, for their collapse in 1940. After all, had there been dry land for Hitler's armies to go as far west as they went east—to Stalingrad—they would have got to what is actually the mid-Atlantic. Western Europe, unfortunately, does not have the space the Russians have. The "collapse" of France in 1940 was, as De Gaulle well said at the time, a defeat in battle. Prussia suffered as bad a defeat by the French at Jena in 1806, was overrun by French cavalry which moved almost as fast as did German motorized troops in 1940, was occupied, and had its collaborators. Yet Prussia was fundamentally sound in 1806, and soon developed its resistance. So, too, the French after the shock of 1940 developed their resistance, which in 1944 gave the Allies very great aid indeed.

I have tried to show that to judge by their actions, by

their actual work, the peoples of Western Europe have displayed since the war a very great ability to come back. But I grant if their activities are, so to speak, merely a set of reflexes, a kind of dogged and unthinking continuance of ways to which they are accustomed, if their activities are uninformed by the kind of adaptive thinking we used to subsume under the concept of "progress," then indeed Europe is as badly off as the pessimists think she is. I do not think the peoples of Western Europe are in anything like this hopeless state of mind.

Now in this broad concluding survey of their actual state of mind I shall somewhat reluctantly make a distinction—not, please note carefully, a clear-cut opposition—between the temper of the intellectuals, the people whose main concern is with words and symbols, and the others, the people whose main concern is with things and their relationships. I say reluctantly because I do not wish to make a false and usually snobbish distinction between intellectual sheep and nonintellectual goats, and because I do not wish to imply that what the artists and thinkers do is quite unrelated to what ordinary people do. But, as we have had to content ourselves with merely skirting the philosophy of history, so we must content ourselves with skirting the even more puzzling subject of the sociology of the intellectual classes. For the present it is enough to note that, for the purposes of a rough analysis of the state of mind of contemporary Western Europeans, a quite undogmatic and flexible empirical distinction between intellectuals and the rest of the people is a convenient tool of thought.

Let us begin with the intellectuals, if only because since they are articulate they are easier, at least on the surface,

to get at. I am willing to agree that this is an Age of
Anxiety, and that no one is likely, if one can judge by its
first half, to write a book about the twentieth century with
a title like that the late F. S. Marvin chose for one on the
nineteenth, *The Century of Hope*. Yet I think it most
important to note that the disciplines from which that
metaphor of anxiety stems, psychology, or even psychiatry,
are very far indeed from gloom and despair. The
psychologist recognizes the existence of anxiety, but he
has by no means given up the attempt to overcome it.
He does not, if he is sensible, think he can overcome it
always and in everybody; but he is no pessimist, nor even
in a derogatory sense, an anti-intellectual. Indeed, Freud
seems to me the legitimate heir of the wiser and subtler
spirits of the eighteenth-century Enlightenment, just as
Marx is the legitimate heir of the shallower and more impatient spirits of that century.

The closest thing to a fashionable belief in postwar times
has been Existentialism, by no means a rosy, happy outlook on life. The existentialists are split into two wings,
the Christian and the non-Christian. The Christian existentialists, in so far as they are Christians, cannot be wholly
pessimistic about man's fate. No doubt some of the followers of Kierkegaard, like the master himself, must seem
to the moderate, earthly outsider wild Christians, Christians
who have tipped toward madness the difficult balance
Christianity has always had to maintain between this world
of the senses and some other world or worlds. But the bulk
of the young people in Western Europe who have been
influenced by the undoubted postwar revival of Christian
faith—a complex matter, by no means adequately described

as existentialist—seem to me well-balanced, anxious to face this harsh world serenely, not disposed to flee it.

The non-Christian existentialists, whose great vogue is French, and whose best-known leaders are Sartre and Camus, do not seem to me to form a major current in the thought of our time; but it is an interesting one, in which I find confirmation of my thesis that the thought of contemporary Western Europe is by no means as pessimistic as it is painted. To be very summary, these men and women are Stoics, rather querulous and therefore incomplete Stoics, but still men and women who refuse to lie down and be run over, whose very querulousness is a sign of their fighting spirit. At bottom they enjoy their suffering —and not really in a perverse sense, but rather in the spirit of "my head is bloody but unbowed." I suspect that at moments they may even forget to suffer, if only in the spirit of the very pessimistic forgotten poet, who once turned upon himself and wrote:

> *Terence, this is stupid stuff:*
> *You eat your victuals fast enough;*
> *There can't be much amiss, 'tis clear,*
> *To see the rate you drink your beer.*

Moreover, some of the simpler and more hopeful faiths still survive, in something of the way A. E. Housman, who of course is not really forgotten, survives. The bright young men today, as usual when they are so described, for the most part actually bright middle-aged men, would not be caught dead with a copy of *A Shropshire Lad*, any more than those of my generation would have been caught dead with a copy of *Evangeline*. Almost certainly many

younger people will live to find that the work of T. S.
Eliot has had the same fate among the *avant-garde* of 1980.
But Eliot will survive fashion. What I am saying is that
in a sense the direct heritage of the Enlightenment, the line
of Voltaire and Jefferson, the Utilitarians and the Fabians,
even though it is by no means the height of intellectual
fashion, remains a living heritage. Lord Russell, if no one
else, should remind us how long-lived that tradition is.

Translated into political terms, this survival of the
tradition of the Enlightenment, enriched and deepened as
I think it has been by our modern awareness of the importance of the irrational—or the nonrational—in human
life and therefore of the necessity of gradualness, means
the survival of the Third Force, the Vital Center, the
moderate but firm democrats. The strength of this force
in Britain and in the small countries of Scandinavia, the
Lowlands, and Switzerland is obvious. In Germany, Italy,
and above all France this force is indeed more obviously
menaced by extremists who in power might set our common
cause back seriously. The recent elections in Italy have
weakened it there, but by no means destroyed it. Even in
these countries the moderate democrats have managed to
cling to power ever since the end of the war, and I think
an unbiased observer would conclude that today they are
at least no weaker over the whole region than they were
eight years ago. Certainly Communism has not made
important converts among the intellectuals anywhere in
the West in the last few years—Sartre, contrary to belief
in some quarters, is no better convert than was André Gide
—nor to judge by the election returns, among the whole
population. The high tide would seem for the present to
be passed.

Modern art remains a puzzle to the social diagnostician. Without going all the way with horrified conservatives I am willing to admit that some of the work of the twentieth-century *avant-garde* does seem to me quite beyond the border of sanity, does seem to me a kind of cultivation of private, quite eccentric experience that can never be absorbed into the common experience of educated men. Yet we must not forget that the history of the arts—I am using the word in the widest sense to include literature as well as the arts—is filled with dead ends now known only to historians of the arts. As I suggested earlier, some of the more shocking innovators of the first part of our century are now safely enshrined as classics. Somehow time does sort out, not perhaps with perfect clarity the good from the bad, but at least the communicable from the uncommunicable. The once very cautious French ministry of fine arts, which used never to risk official exhibits of contemporary arts, has now housed on the Avenue du Président Wilson (no, they haven't changed the name) a most interesting collection which comes right down to the day before yesterday. As a mere layman with perhaps too strong a desire not to be illiberal in these matters, I was struck with how much of this work held my interest, seemed indeed to give me the encouraging feeling that I could understand a little of what it was all about. I am quite sure that many paintings and statues there exhibited will not be exhibited in 2053. But much of what was hopefully exhibited in 1853 is fortunately not around to bore or disturb us in 1953. The failures of 1853, I grant you, are not Dadaist or Abstractionist failures. But that is only to say the obvious, that ours is in the arts a more daringly experimental age than was the Victorian. It still seems possible, indeed probable, that some of our experiments have been successful ones. And the dead do not make experiments—not at least of the kind we mortals can analyze here on earth.

In a wider sense than is given by art and literature, the culture of contemporary Western Europe shows a clear vitality, the ability to achieve outstanding, new things. We Americans sometimes take an attitude which infuriates us when we find it among the Russians—that of assuming we have a natural monopoly of the first places in everything from science to sport. This is not so; the list of firsts for Western Europe in our own time is not to be forgotten. It was the British who brought to first fruit radar and the jet airplane, however much we Americans have done to develop them. German inventiveness we are less likely to question, and we have made full use of it since we defeated them.

The French we are likely to dismiss as quite burned out. Yet the French have just set up at Mont-Louis in the Pyrenees the first major pilot plant for the direct use of sun power; and they have just finished at Donzère-Mondragon on the Rhône a great hydroelectric plant which, by diverting the river into a canal, avoids the drowning of good farming land in a great reservoir subject to the difficulties of silting-up. French science has suffered from French economic and political difficulties, as has French scholarship, but neither are at as low an ebb as many Americans assume. French physics and French economics are not at the moment very distinguished; French biology remains at a very high creative level. The "school of Paris" is getting old—most of its painters who are still living are septuagenarians at least—but Paris is still a very great center of painting. Nor has Hollywood, in spite of the claims of

American periodicals, by any means replaced Paris as the center of fashions for women. As for what Hollywood really symbolizes, we need not here repeat the endless complaints of American intellectuals against our moving pictures. Sufficient to note that the Europeans have a lively, interesting movie industry of their own, and that they can sometimes out-Hollywood Hollywood itself, as well as turn out such subtle and wholly unsentimental pictures as the recent French *Jeux Interdits*.

The American who "keeps up with" what is going on in the world of culture still has to pay great attention to what is going on in Europe. The cultural balance, like the political and the economic balance, has certainly swung our way, but it is a balance, and no contrast between everything and nothing. What the historian of ideas will eventually make of Existentialism we cannot know. But it is surely the most important philosophical movement since the war, and it is essentially European—German and French—in origin. In the fine arts, in music, in literature, in the lesser arts, European names still fill the pages of the critical journals all over the world. Our age may be degenerate, Alexandrian or worse, but we are all Alexandrians together in the West. We Americans cannot claim absolute domination, not even as hopeless neurotics, or materialists, or makers of the wastelands of the soul.

One more word before I leave the intellectuals. An American who moves about in intellectual circles in Western Europe is, unless he is much more thick-skinned than we usually are, bound to feel uncomfortable. These people make little effort to disguise the fact that they distrust and fear the United States. There are quite obvious reasons why they feel this way. They have directly suffered the ravages of war, and we have not. They envy our obvious prosperity. They resent the patronizing attitude many Americans abroad all too often assume. They resent, being only human, our very generosity toward them. They are afraid we are about to enter the kind of career of expansion their own history has shown that great victorious nations have so often entered. Above all, I think, since they are intellectuals who prize the traditional refinements, they tend to think of us as essentially vulgar and tasteless, as, if I may speak symbolically, about to force upon them Coca-Cola and destroy their wines.

All this comes out neatly in a postwar German novel by Maria von Kirchbach, called *Cupid in Khaki*. Its heroine, whose husband has been made prisoner of war, is besieged by an American officer in the forces of occupation. He offers her all the riches of the Post Exchange, all the little luxuries she has had so long to do without. She is sorely tempted, but it is fair to say that her tempter behaves quite honorably, for an American. At the right moment, the husband comes back from Russian captivity, and the wife, putting European spirituality and *douceur de vivre* ahead of crass American materialism, decides to stay with her husband. This attitude, even among the most aesthetically inclined, is not without its amusing ambivalence, for the very same ones who declare we are all Babbitts or worse also have the greatest respect for Hemingway and Faulkner, even for Steinbeck and Damon Runyan. Part of the trouble is that they suffer from cultural lag. European intellectuals tend to think of the United States as our own intellectuals thought of it in the 1920's. They are still back with Sinclair Lewis and Mr. H. L. Mencken. We ourselves are thus not altogether without responsibility for their opinion of us. Time, we may hope, will remedy this lag.

Many American liberals are so hostile to nationalism—except among colonial peoples—and so distrustful of the commonplaces of nationalism in general, that they will not face the obvious. But it seems inescapably true, as such analogies go, that we feel very differently about criticism from within the family and from without. We take what Sinclair Lewis and Mr. Mencken, what Mr. Lewis Mumford and Miss Hortense Powdermaker have to say about our crudities in our stride, but we bristle when an Englishman or a Frenchman says the same things. This is a fact of life, a law of nature, and the best we can do is allow for it. We can indeed try to see that Europeans learn about our good points as well as about our bad ones, and this our State Department is trying hard to do, under heavy fire from within the country, as it always is.

Our propaganda—for such it is—runs among European intellectuals up against their preconceived notions of the United States as a vast Hollywood, and against their distrust of all propaganda not directly stamped by the tradition of intellectual revolt. Their attitude is hard for us to understand sympathetically, but we must make the effort. After all, I must repeat, they are simply saying what our own intellectuals said about us a generation ago, and what some of them are still saying.

Politically this distrust of the United States takes among the West European intellectual classes rather the form of "neutralism" than that of actual siding with Russia against us. The neutralist feels like Mercutio, victim of the struggle between Montagues and Capulets—"a plague o' both your houses." It is not a noble feeling, nor has it a sound logical basis in history. The spiritual crisis of our age has roots in Western Europe at least as deep as in the United States and Russia. Most reflective Europeans know this quite well. But the war was fought there, not here, and we should realize that Mercutio's response is a most human one. Some of us Americans have made this response even today, and it looks in the perspective of history as if Americans collectively made a very similar response in 1919, when we were quite willing to abandon all Europe to its Montagues and Capulets.

Nor should we close our minds to the possibility that European neutralism, *in its milder and more sensible forms*, may be a force for good in our divided world. The concept of an honest broker, a mediator between the two extremes, is one many Americans, in the midst of this cold-hot war, find most unpalatable. We don't need an umpire —this is no game. But in calmer moments we may bring ourselves to admit that not all compromise is appeasement. Here the Western Europeans, working within the United Nations, may yet help bring about a new and more satisfactory Locarno. There *is* a difference between compromise and appeasement, however tricky that distinction may seem to the confirmed semanticist, and the Europeans are perhaps better placed than we are to help bring that difference out concretely.

The ordinary man, as I have already suggested, does not altogether reflect the dislike and distrust of the United States common, though by no means universal, among European intellectuals. He may, and if he is a Communist he certainly does, fear us as a possible aggressor. But he does not share the intellectual's distrust of our material achievements. Indeed, he would like to have some of them for himself. I do not think he has taken overly much to Coca-Cola, but he would certainly like a Chevrolet, or a television set, or a house with all the latest improvements. And, to the horror of the intellectuals, he seems to like American movies. Indeed, I think it fair to say that the European man in the street looks at us with admiration mixed with envy. But it is not a searing envy, not indeed a hopeless envy, and my net impression is that on the whole he thinks quite a lot better of us than of the Russians. This, as I shall shortly point out, is confirmed by the pollers of public opinion.

Our real interest in the average Western European, however, should be in his feelings about his own prospects and the future of his society. The man in the street has opinions, and ultimately in all these societies can if he votes together in a mass swing the fate of Western Europe. He need not vote, indeed, but only acquiesce. It is rather more than a half-truth—perhaps a four-fifths truth—that a people gets the government it wants, or perhaps deserves. If the European masses are apathetic, resigned to sullen submission, unwilling to work, quietly desperate, then they are headed for dictatorship of the Right. If they are actively indignant at what they think the injustice of the ruling classes, if they feel an explosive hatred toward the government, if they are also full of energy, they are headed toward a revolution which I think in these days can only lead to dictatorship of the Left.

Yet the state of mind of the average man is hard to test objectively. The mere traveler's impressions must always be suspect, and the formal study of public opinion is, as a social science, still in its beginnings. Yet there are promising beginnings. The systematic study of the press, interviews with escaped Europeans, the cautious use of cloak-and-dagger sources, together with a good background knowledge of the societies studied, enabled the Americans and the British to estimate with surprising accuracy the way their armies would be received on the continent in 1944. To such sources the professional student of public opinion can now add the public-opinion polls. These polls, which incidentally would appear to be part of our American contribution to the culture of the West, now exist in most of the countries of free Europe and are federated into a World Association for Public Opinion Research. In many circles it is fashionable to sneer at the pollsters, but I think no one conscientiously interested in the truth about human behavior on this earth can afford such a sneer. Most of these research workers are aware that a scientist would indeed be a faker if he made no mistakes.

I shall here confine myself to a few mere scraps of testing from France, which after all does seem to be the country most seared by the horrors of our time. *Sondages* ("Samplings" or "Soundings"), the organ of the Institut Français d'Opinion Publique, a very active group in French academic life, is a fascinating record of French public opinion on most varied subjects. Its polls are sharpest, perhaps, when concentrated on questions of political measures, domestic and international, but it also goes on to wider if vaguer questions of man's fate. In 1951, for example, *Sondages* conducted a poll on private worries, and discovered the not surprising fact that more people worried—or admitted worrying—about money than about any other single matter. But in a breakdown by classes, the well-to-do in October 1949 showed 33 per cent worrying most about money, the middle class 52 per cent, the lower middle class 63 per cent, the poor 63 per cent. Americans with stereotypes about France may be surprised to learn that worrying about love affairs, which was not even separately listed, but buried among "personal and health problems," could achieve in September 1951 only a second place of 10 per cent. "Uncertainty about the future" could do no better than tie for fifth place with 6 per cent. But these soundings are likely to be destructive of our simpler stereotypes about the French. A study of opinion about Paris, both among Parisians and provincials, is full of interesting details. I note that in the provinces 30 per cent admitted envying their relatives or friends in Paris, but 65 per cent stated that they did not envy them. Of course, they may have been lying, the curse of all these polls; but I have always suspected the notion that every Frenchman would live in Paris if he could. I can mention but one more detail, a French poll of August 1950, after the outbreak of the Korean War. There were in sympathy with the United States 52 per cent, in sympathy with Russia 13 per cent. You may wonder about the remaining 35 per cent. Well, 18 per cent "ne se prononcent pas," do not answer, a not surprising percentage in a question as sharp as this, and 17 per cent made "other responses," which I guess to have been variations on Mercutio's "a plague o' both your houses."

We cannot linger any longer over these details, which I suggest add up to an alert, active, disputatious people, but not to one on the verge of a collective nervous breakdown. We may take it as typical of the characteristic French diversity of opinion that 30 per cent of parents polled were for compulsory Latin for their children, 28 per cent were against it, and 42 per cent were in a position that suggests to me that French parents are weakening, getting Americanized—they were "undecided."

Sport deserves a serious word. There is no good sociology of sport, no doubt because those who know most about sociology know little about sport, and those who know most about sport know little about sociology. But Americans in particular, if they are not intellectuals, are likely to estimate athletic achievement as at least a kind of index of the vitality of a group. Here our national assumption of superiority is pretty complete. Europeans, many of us think, simply can't compete with us. Certainly we always manage, at least by the unofficial point scores our reporters make, to win the Olympic games. But even in sports, the American advantage is only a comparative one. The Europeans manage to hold up their end.

Indeed, in some respects European sport seems in a healthier state than in this country. Their professional sport, like ours, exists to make money for its promoters, to give the public a chance to gamble, and by no means just incidentally, to satisfy the pride, the pooled self-esteem, of a group, local, regional, or national. Neither the purely commercial side, nor the gambling side, nor the gladiatorial side—the subsidized few playing for the amusement of the many spectators—of professional sports are very different in Western Europe from what they are in this country. It is, however, in amateur sport that the West Europeans seem today, on the whole, rather nearer the conventional ideals of sport for sport's sake, of widespread actual play, than we do. Golf is far less popular, save perhaps in Britain, than here. Tennis, on the other hand, is played a great deal in Western Europe. Amateur team sports in Europe have never been as closely identified with higher education as in America. Soccer, which is for Europeans what baseball is for us, rugby, field hockey, basketball, and in Britain alone, cricket, are all played by innumerable clubs organized specifically for play, and identified with a great variety of neighborhood, vocational, class, even religious groups. One result is that the West European young man does not stop team play at twenty-one or twenty-two when he graduates from college, and content himself with golf, tennis, or squash thereafter. He keeps right on with his club, often well into middle age.

European nationalism finds a steady outlet in sport. The neutral spectator at an international soccer match between France and Germany, say—relations were resumed in 1952 with France winning the first match—may well doubt whether such contests do in fact lessen national antagonisms. Certainly he will take in a somewhat ironic sense the notion that international team sports fulfill William James's call for a "moral equivalent of war." Yet here as so often the idealist asks for too much. To judge by the behavior of the crowds—and the writings of sports reporters afterward—a good deal of what in present-day cant terms is called "aggression" does get taken out in ways much less violent than actual warfare. International sport as it now is in Western Europe may not be an effective sublimation of aggressive drives; but it is at least a partial satisfaction—since even the little countries can sometimes beat the big ones at soccer—of the pooled self-esteem of nationalism.

Perhaps it is just as well that, except for the Olympic games, which come only once in four years, and tennis, which remains pretty genteel in spite of the crowd appeal of Davis Cup matches, we Americans do not compete with

Europeans on a national basis in team sports with mass spectators. Our national drive in such activities would doubtless push us to the top rather too much of the time for a Europe that likes to have the spoils well shared. As it is, we go on playing among ourselves alone our peculiar kind of football, in which foot and ball meet with increasing rareness; and we play baseball with no more international competition than that afforded by an occasional Japanese or Caribbean team. Of course, it would take us some time to polish up our soccer, and practically learn rugby and cricket, in order to compete with European countries in these sports, and at first we might be soundly beaten—something that in Bentham's terms would certainly bring the greatest happiness to the greatest number. For there is no doubt that the ordinary European, if he does not hate us as do some intellectuals, is a bit tired of our eternal successes.

Still, as one looks over the complex activities men label "sport," the likenesses, the identities indeed, between Americans and Western Europeans stand out perhaps even more sharply than they do in what we commonly think of as higher forms of culture. A fan is a fan everywhere, even in England, where if cricket crowds are decorous, soccer crowds are not. But the easy test is the journalism of sport, which shows but slightly the stamp of national character. Sports writers everywhere go in for elegant variation, pumped-up drama, and critical attitudes which suggest that most of them, in France and Britain as in the United States, are good sound intellectuals and should have columns of their own. If there is a difference in man playing in the United States and in Western Europe, it is slight, very slight, and sociologically not really important. It is tempting to find Europeans at play a little less tense than we are, a little less

painfully self-conscious heirs of Hercules, a little more serene. Europeans, and especially Frenchmen, fish happily
without ever catching a fish, and apparently without ex-
pecting to. We Americans want to catch the legal limit or
a bit more, or get the fish and game commissioner out of
office. Few Frenchmen would even in literature identify
the fisherman with Prometheus, as Melville and Hemingway
do; Loti's *Pêcheur d'Islande* is a quiet fellow indeed beside
Captain Ahab and Hemingway's old man of the sea.

But here again the eternal difficulty of generalization in
such matters crops up. If sport is at one extreme team competition before mass spectators, at the other it is one man or
a few climbing a mountain, diving under the sea, sailing a
raft across the ocean. It is adventure, exploration, the assault
on the unknown—and the breaking of a record. There is
nothing very serene, quiet, or even very sensible, about
most of these activities and a Voltaire or a Shaw has always
had fun with these heaven-stormers. But Heartbreak House
never really understands Horseback Hall. The most con-
secrated of sportmen, the mountain climbers, are almost
always themselves intellectuals, members of Heartbreak
House. In our Western tradition, the adventurer, the ex-
plorer, *le recordman* (the word unbelievably is French), is
surely associated with life, with the Promethean spark. In
these days of Everest and Annapurna, of the Kon-Tiki
expedition, and many more instances of man struggling
heroically if not without publicity against fate, Europe
would seem to be very much alive indeed, more alive than
we are. But these are honors we may well leave to the
Europeans. After all, we Americans allowed the adven-
turous French and Spaniards to explore the interior of
North America; we merely peopled it.

I should like to conclude with what I regard as decisive

evidence that the peoples of Western Europe are not losing their hold on life. Back in the 1930's the demographers were sure the population curve in Western Europe and in the United States was flattening out. Now they know that there was immediately after the war a sharp rise in the birth rate, a rise certainly far greater than the normal postwar rise from postponed marriages and return of husbands, and not really anticipated by the experts.

A final statistical table is called for here. The source is the *Demographic Yearbook, 1952* (Statistical Office of the United Nations, New York, 1952, pp. 224–231).

Table 3.   Crude Birth Rates

	1937	1949
Austria	12.8	16.3
Belgium	15.4	17.2
Denmark	18.0	18.9
France	15.0	20.9
Ireland	19.2	21.5
Italy	22.9	20.4
Netherlands	19.8	23.7
Norway	15.0	19.5
Spain	22.7	21.7
United Kingdom	15.3	17.0
United States	17.1	24.0

The curve is now flattening out a bit, but we are still far from the rates of the 1930's over most of Western society. Now I see no way you can account for all these babies except by giving up a position of extreme pessimism as to the temper of the parents. One European intellectual with whom I discussed this point did indeed argue that the rise in birth rate is a sign of despair; people no longer give a damn, they are sunk in sensuality, and anyway the welfare state will take care of the children. Surely this assertion is almost a caricature of the intellectual's unwillingness to get beyond what his emotions dictate to his deductive processes. If you incline, as so many of our supposedly anti-Marxists do, to the economic interpretation of human motivation, you will say that we are in prosperous times—even in dying Western Europe—and that of course the birth rate rises. But this is at least an admission that we *are* in prosperous times. If you incline to Freudian or similar psychological interpretations, you may say that this generation has come to feel that contraception is unduly repressive and inhibiting, that the one-child family is cruelty to the only child, that at least two or three children are necessary for the parents' ids, libidos, or just plain human nature. If you incline to put great emphasis on the postwar revival of religious orthodoxy and moral seriousness, you have still another explanation for the rise in the birth rate. You may, if you like hard-boiled simplicity, say that we have large families in the middle classes just because our parents had small ones. If you believe that in such great social phenomena we must always deal with multiple causation, you may say that all these explanations, and others we have not touched upon, are factors in the end result. You will not, however, find it easy to explain this renewal of life as in itself a sure sign of approaching death.

We come at the end of this study by no means to the unfashionable—and unsound—conclusion that this is the best of possible worlds in Western Europe. On the contrary, we know that Europeans are facing heavy burdens and difficult problems. But we know, first, what I have throughout rather implied by occasional cross-references to the United States than brought out explicitly, that these burdens and these problems are not limited to Western Europe, but are basically shared with us; they are the common burdens and problems of the free Western world, from which we Americans are by no means exempt. And we know, second, that Europeans are for the most part not laying down the burdens and dodging the problems, but are facing their future with courage and resourcefulness. My slanting reference immediately above to Dr. Pangloss's optimism about the "best of possible worlds" carries my incurably historical imagination back to his creator. Voltaire's *Candide* is a bitter satire, and his hero's woes could hardly have been greater in our century than in his own. Yet in the end, you will remember, Candide decides that "il faut cultiver notre jardin"—we must cultivate our garden. This the Europeans are now doing. It is still a fine garden, and they are still good gardeners.

I would not, however, end on so subdued a note. There is resignation, acceptance of this world in Western Europe, but there is also the lift of courage and hope. Honegger, the French composer, by origin a Swiss, was one of those Parisians who cultivated their gardens through the gloomy months after the fall of France in 1940. His "Symphony for String Orchestra" was finished in the autumn of 1941. It is a quiet work—quiet certainly for the composer of "Pacific 231" and "Rugby"—perhaps a bit remote, and not an obvious program piece. But at the very end of the last movement, the trumpets, hitherto silent and unnoticed as the strings play on, burst suddenly into a simple and very moving chorale. I cannot think of a Voltairian chorale, nor indeed of an Existentialist chorale. Honegger's trumpets called in that year of Nazi triumph to something deeper and older in the human spirit than anything the mere social scientist can put into words. They are still calling, still heard. You can hear them, if you will, even above the very great noise the prophets of doom are making.

Take My Word for It

OTHER BOOKS BY VERNON PIZER

Glorious Triumphs: Athletes Who Conquered Adversity
Shortchanged by History: America's Neglected Innovators
You Don't Say: How People Communicate Without Speech
Ink, Ark., and All That: How American Places Got Their Names
The United States Army
The World Ocean: Man's Last Frontier
The Useful Atom (with William R. Anderson)
Rockets, Missiles and Space

Take
My Word

for It

CARL A. RUDISILL LIBRARY
LENOIR RHYNE COLLEGE

VERNON PIZER

DODD, MEAD & COMPANY · NEW YORK

422
P68x
124922
may 1983

Copyright © 1981 by Vernon Pizer
All rights reserved
No part of this book may be reproduced in any form
without permission in writing from the publisher
Printed in the United States of America

1 2 3 4 5 6 7 8 9 10

Library of Congress Cataloging in Publication Data

Pizer, Vernon, date
Take my word for it.

Includes index.
1. English language—Eponyms. 2. Biography. I. Title.
PE1596.P59   422   81-43226
ISBN 0-396-07986-5   AACR2

For Billy and Camille,

for so many reasons

Contents

Take My Word for It

1

Men of Their Word

A popular landmark in present-day London is Marble Arch at the northeast corner of Hyde Park. With the great Arch framed against the park's greenery, it is an attractive spot. But it was not always so. At a much earlier time it was a grim and grisly place known as Tyburn, location of the public gallows. There were not many days when cutthroats from Newgate prison or public figures who had offended the crown did not swing from the end of the hangman's rope.

Of all the executioners who presided at the gallows during Tyburn's six centuries of existence there was not another quite like Godfrey Derrick (listed in some surviving records as "Derick"). Only a few months before he became Tyburn's hangman in 1600, Derrick had been arrested in the French city of Calais on a charge of rape. Tried and found guilty, he was sentenced to be hanged. Desperate to escape the noose, Derrick pulled every string possible to have the British authorities intercede on his behalf. Through an intermediary his plight was brought to the attention of Robert, Earl of Essex, who secured Derrick's release and his return to England where he obtained the executioner's post at Tyburn. So, his neck having been saved from one end of the rope, he now placed his hand on the other end.

Tyburn and Derrick seemed made for each other. Warming to his task, the new hangman studied the gallows—a simple affair of three long legs arranged so that a rope could be suspended where their tops joined—and figured out a way to make his performance smoother and easier. Fixing a beam horizontally from the top of the gallows, he moved the rope out to the end of the beam. Now he could do his victims in without having the legs of the structure get in his way. Never before had the condemned been dispatched in so businesslike a fashion.

Godfrey Derrick had been manipulating the rope at Tyburn for little more than a year when one of the condemned brought before him was a nobleman who had fallen from grace—Robert, Earl of Essex, the very man who had saved him from a French noose. If he had no stomach for the task, Derrick hid it well. He strung up the Earl of Essex with his usual brisk efficiency.

Soon everyone began calling the Tyburn gallows "the derrick" after the hangman who was so single-mindedly devoted to the lethal device. In time the word came to mean any lifting apparatus. Thus, Godfrey Derrick became more than simply Tyburn's most notorious executioner; he became an eponym—the source of a word that is derived from a person's name.

Eponyms and the name-words that derive from them are what this book is all about.

Eponyms took root almost as soon as proper names themselves were first devised. If mythology had not included Morpheus as the god of dreams, then narcotics agents today would be seizing a drug called something other than morphine. Because Caesar ruled ancient Rome with a fist of iron, his name became the source of two terms for an autocratic leader: czar and kaiser. And ever since pre-Biblical antiquity, drastic, harsh measures have been known as draconian measures because Draco, compiler of the first written legal code of ancient Athens, specified death as punishment for even minor crimes. The Bible itself is a rich source of eponyms—from Nimrod, who was so great a hunter that marksmen ever since have been called nimrods, to Jonah whose misfortune in being swallowed by a whale causes ill-fated persons to be known as jonahs.

Though the process of deriving words from proper names dates back to the distant past, the term "eponym" is only little more than a century old. It was coined from two Greek words, *epi* and *onyma,* whose literal meaning is "upon a name." But it was formed for the broader purpose of meaning "the person for whom something is named." There is often a tendency today to use the term to mean the thing that is named rather than the person for whom the thing is named. However, in these pages eponyms will continue to be what they were meant to be when the term was created: persons from whom name-words are derived.

But if this book is about eponyms and their name-words, it is not about just any eponym or any name-word. This book is not simply a *collection;* it is a *selection.* There would be little gain in dwelling on the commonplace and the already familiar, or the unremarkable and the juiceless, or the highly specialized expression restricted to use by a relatively small group. So scant attention, if any at all, will be paid to such eponyms and their name-words as Louis Pasteur and pasteurization and James Bowie and the bowie knife, or to the pair of Italian anatomists—Gabriele Fallopio and Bartolomeo Eustachio—whom medicine memorializes in its fallopian and eustachian tubes, or to the trio of brilliant physicists from whose names are derived ampere and ohm and volt. The real rewards in the world of eponymy come from concentrating on those that cause an eyebrow to rise in wonder or a mouth to turn up in a smile, that shed fresh light in a fresh way, that have a story behind them that merits the telling.

For instance, take young Prince Charles Phillipe de Condé, grandnephew of Louis XIII, King of France in the early seventeenth century. Passionately fond of sweets, almost from the moment he could toddle about the palace by himself, the young prince made his way to the royal kitchens to beg for sugary confections. At first his performance amused the kitchen staff and they rewarded him with all the sweets he craved. But then the master chef, Vincent de la Chapelle, became alarmed when he realized that the youngster's constant eating of sweets and his neglect of more nutritious foods could damage his health. How does one refuse a royal request, even from such a youthful member of royalty?

The chef hit upon an ingenious solution to his dilemma. Selecting nourishing foods—meats, vegetables, fruits—he prepared them with an enticing glaze made of sugar, egg whites, and chopped nuts. With eyes only for the sweet coating, the boy was in this way lured into eating what he would otherwise pass up. King Louis came across the glazed dishes one day, sampled them, and smacked his lips in appreciation. He questioned the chef about his new creation. Delighted by the story of their invention, Louis ordered that the sweet glaze be named for the young member of the de Condé family who had caused its birth. So de Condé became the eponymous source of "candied" dishes. Later, when public appetite grew for the sweet coating without the filling it had originally been intended to cover, it was called candy.

Closer to home there is Philadelphia, a city that appeared to have the golden touch in the early nineteenth century. Its industries thrived, its bank vaults were stuffed, its architects and artisans were busy erecting grand mansions for its legion of business tycoons.

To the careful observer, however, there were signs that some of those giants of Philadelphia's business affairs may have become spoiled by their success; some had grown complacent—having scaled the heights, they seemed to be losing a little of their drive. Not so one merchant, a distiller who turned out a sound whiskey and promoted it vigorously. His whiskey bottles with bright labels prominently displaying his name—E. G. Booze—became a commonplace sight all over the region. An army of drinkers bellied up to a multitude of bars to call for Booze. In time E. G.'s business was overtaken and outdistanced by competing distillers, eventually losing out to its rivals and passing from the scene. But by then booze, with a small "b," had become a firmly fixed name-word in the language of America.

By odd coincidence, booze was soon joined by a second, equally enduring Americanism for whiskey and it, too, was derived from a proper name, although in this case its eponymous source was a place rather than a person. The new term came out of Alaska where no prospector ventured into the wilderness without his sourdough starter to enable him to prepare dough for his bread. One group of miners, a little more inventive than the rest, discovered that if they permitted their sourdough to ferment fully they could extract an exceedingly potent drink from the liquid rising to the top. The place where they found that sourdough could be drink as well as food was called Hooch-in-noo by the local Tlingit Indians. Because strong drink was a scarce commodity in the Alaska of that era, the news spread fast and before long prospectors throughout the territory were making their own "hooch" and the vocabulary had gained a new word.

If booze and hooch followed curious paths toward enduring niches among the hundreds of name-words that add spice to the language, their saga is closely rivaled by a more recent newcomer: Frisbee. According to some authorities on the folklore of these popular, pint-sized flying saucers, it all began on the Yale campus in 1827 when an undergraduate named Elihu Frisbee, rebelling against compulsory chapel attendance, hurled the collection plate out across the lawn. Others supposedly took up the plate-scaling as a sport, labeling their missiles Frisbees in honor of the initiator. This story is too glib to ring true, though it seems clear that Yale has close links to the birth of the Frisbee.

The account put forth by another, and larger, body of Frisbee historians is more credible. In this version the whole thing began with the Frisbies, a family of bakers in Bridgeport, Connecticut, in the 1930s and 1940s. During their lunch break the truck drivers of the Frisbie Pie Company amused themselves by scaling the tin pie plates across the bakery yard. Students at nearby Yale picked up pie plate-scaling from the drivers, and from the Yale campus the game migrated to Princeton and other Ivy League colleges. Unable to survive the dislocations of World War II, the pie company faltered and finally closed, but by then plate-scaling was a fixture at Yale and its sister colleges. In the 1950s Fred Morrison, an alert Californian who had spotted the campus craze, began manufacturing the flying discs out of plastic, copyrighting Frisbee as the official name in deference to the Frisbie family whose pie plates had spawned them. After that, Frisbees soared into the skies nationwide and into the language.

One of the enduring fascinations of eponymy is that it is so lively, so continuously enriched by the arrival of new eponyms and their derivative name-words. It is an ongoing process that shows no signs of letting up. Among some of the newer arrivals are the fanatical U.S. senator who abused his position, giving the world McCarthyism as a synonym for political witchhunting, John Taliaferro Thompson who invented the weapon that made tommygun a part of the modern vocabulary, George Gallup who has made polling a preoccupation of modern society, thereby leading Europeans to refer to public opinion polls as gallups, and Walter Cronkite whose international reputation in newscasting causes Sweden to use cronkiter as a term for TV anchormen.

Occasionally a name-word turns out not to have the stamina for the long haul and so it has a brief life and then fades away. Like shaddock, a fruit named for the sea captain who introduced it into the Caribbean Islands in the eighteenth century from seed he had obtained on a voyage to the East Indies. Cultivation of the fruit he brought back thrives in the New World, but now it is known as grapefruit. And sometimes, though the name-word flourishes, it is the eponymous inspiration for it that falls through the cracks of history. Like sequins, the shiny discs used to decorate dresses and named for the obscure French chemist who created them first as tiny artificial flowers and about whom no records remain.

If there is one certainty surrounding eponyms it is that they are a notably varied lot. They range all the way from Venus, the ancient Roman goddess of love from whom come two distinctly opposite name-words; venereal and venerable, to Vidkun Quisling, the Norwegian turncoat whose collaboration with the Nazis in World War II gave the dictionary quisling as a synonym for a renegade. From Mausolus of Caria, Near Eastern ruler in the fourth century

B.C. whose enormous tomb was one of the Seven Wonders of the World and created mausoleum as a term for a burial structure, and from another of the Seven Wonders, the Colossus of Rhodes, gigantic bronze statue that inspired the design of the Statue of Liberty and gave the language two words, colossal and coliseum, to Samuel A. Maverick, Texas rancher in the early 1800s who refused to brand his cattle and allowed them to range freely, so that maverick became a term for any unorthodox individual who deviates from the customary way of doing things. (One of Samuel's descendants, Maury Maverick, mayor of San Antonio in the 1940s, also enlarged the vocabulary when he coined gobbledygook as a derisive term for bureaucratic double-talk.) And from Stentor, leather-lunged herald at the Seige of Troy, from whom comes stentorian as a name-word for loud-voiced; to Titian, the superb Venetian artist who used color so masterfully that his name was given to the subtle shading achieved by blending, red, brown and gold; and to Levi Strauss, the German who immigrated to California during the Gold Rush, made sturdy canvas work pants for the miners, and in the process put the world into blue jeans and levis into the dictionary.

Words—how could we exist without them? They are the indispensable tools that enable us to communicate with one another. In that sense, a word is a mechanical device in the same way that a valve is a mechanical device. Manipulate valves and fluids will flow between two points; manipulate words and communication will flow between two minds. But name-words are different from ordinary words. They are special, more than simply links in the chain of language that connects one mind to another. They stand apart from and loom above other words because they are linguistic memorials to their eponymous sources, to the saints and the sinners, to the wise men and the fools, to the blue bloods and the commoners who inspired them.

Behind each eponym lies a story, a tale of human comedy or of tragedy, of folly or triumph, of selfishness or selflessness. In them one can glimpse the ever-changing human parade with its surprises, its humor, its stumbles, and its progress. A voyage among the name-words to discover their eponymous sources and the stories behind them is a rewarding journey, never dull or humdrum, always a new, different, and colorful port to sail into. Many of those ports lie ahead to be explored in the pages that follow.

2

Rank and File

One of the characteristics shared by many whose names have worked their way into the language is that they made their mark, for better or for worse, in the military. There is no apparent reason why so many who bear arms should wind up as eponyms, but ever since antiquity the generals and the admirals and the men they command have been fruitful sources of name-words.

One of the early military eponyms was the king of Epirus in what is now Greece. In 280 B.C. he gathered together his army and led it westward to challenge the Romans. After some minor skirmishing he defeated a major Roman force at Asculum in 279 but it was a hard-fought encounter in which he was compelled to sacrifice a massive number of his own soldiers. So many casualties were sustained by his army in chalking up its victory that it became a weak and demoralized force incapable of pressing on against the enemy.

Reluctantly facing up to reality, the king of Epirus had no alternative to turning his decimated army around and leading it limping back to Greece in humiliating retreat. Ever since then a victory gained at so great a price that the cost is crushing has been known as a Pyrrhic victory, for Pyrrhus, the hapless king who won his battle and lost his war. Inglorious in victory, Pyrrhus was also inglorious in death; he died of head injuries when he was struck by a roof tile hurled by an angry woman.

Eight centuries after the king of Epirus was undone by the battle he won, a new name-word emerged from another military challenge to the Romans. This time the victory gained by the invaders was not Pyrrhic. The aggressors, a fierce Germanic tribe, overwhelmed Rome, routing the city's defenders in utter defeat. Then the triumphant tribesmen rampaged through the city, burning, looting, and brutalizing the inhabitants. Out of this wanton destruction emerged a new entry for the dictionary—vandalism—for the pillaging Vandal tribe.

The wild marauding of the Vandals was something that Colonel Jean Martinet would never have tolerated. Order, precision, rigid discipline were the military gods he worshipped. Unfortunately, he was almost alone in the pew because few others in the seventeenth-century French army shared his convictions. When a new minister was appointed in 1660 to oversee France's military affairs, he looked at the slipshod, poorly organized, and poorly led army and threw up his hands in despair. Turning to Martinet, the minister ordered him to whip the army into shape.

Martinet was the right man for the job. Plunging into the

task with energy and a keen sense of what distinguishes an army from an unruly mob, he devised systems of organization and sequences of drills that would, with only minor change, become the standard for all European armies. He drove his troops hard, demanding maximum effort from them and refusing to accept anything less than instant obedience and a polished performance. By the time he died in 1672 (when accidentally struck by his own artillery while leading an infantry assault in the seige of Duisberg in Germany), the French army had become a disciplined, rationally organized force. It is fitting that martinet remains as a name-word for a rigorous, no-nonsense taskmaster.

However, it isn't only those who actually bear the arms who seem so often to use the military as a pathway to eponymical immortality. Those who furnish those arms also turn out to be fertile ground in which name-words take root readily. Richard Jordan Gatling is a case in point.

There was nothing in his early years to suggest that Gatling would ever be linked to weapons or to wars. Born in North Carolina in 1818, he was gentle, soft-spoken, and introspective. His father, a farmer, continually tinkered with his agricultural implements, trying to improve them and to design new equipment capable of performing a useful function, and this urge to tinker and to innovate rubbed off on the boy. Like his father, he had nimble fingers and a quick, imaginative mind. Between them, father and son invented a machine to sow cotton seed and a second one to thin out cotton plants. Later, on his own, young Gatling devised a machine to sow rice. In 1844 he left North Carolina for St. Louis where he redesigned his rice machine so that it would

sow wheat and where he opened a small shop to manufacture the device.

Gatling soon discovered that the life of a factory owner
held little appeal for him; the routine sameness of each day
brought boredom. So he turned his back on St. Louis and
struck out restlessly in a sequence of strange moves. He
went first to Cincinnati where he entered medical school.
Two years later he withdrew from medical school and
moved on to Indianapolis to try his hand successively, but
not successfully, in railroad and real estate ventures. Next,
he returned to his first love—working with machines. Several improved farm implements came from his creative
mind and skilled hands; the most promising of them was a
steam-operated plow.

The outbreak of the Civil War in 1861 put the final and
most curious twist in Gatling's nomadic life. As the war's
casualties began to appear on the streets—the sightless, the
amputees, the scarred and maimed—he was horrified by
their plight. Sorrowing over this bitter harvest of the
battlefield, he resolved to find a way to halt the ravages of
war. The solution he conceived was, like the man himself,
unusual. He concluded that the best way to rule out war was
to make it so deadly that men and nations would abandon
armed conflict as a way to settle disputes. So the mission of
this gentle man became the creation of more deadly
weapons in the belief that their very lethality would bar
their use.

Immersing himself in the technology of ballistics and
ordnance, he had by late 1862 invented a revolutionary gun
mounting several barrels fixed to a rotating drum. Turning

a crank swiveled the drum around to bring each barrel up into firing position in rapid succession; simultaneously, bullets were fed into the firing mechanism, so that the weapon could discharge a deadly hail of lead at a rate never before attainable. The initial model was crude but the principle of the Gatling gun was sound. Later models incorporated refinements that made it a reliable mass killer. Thus, the kindly inventor so filled with compassion for humanity brought a new order of inhumanity to combat by creating the machine gun. In the years that followed, gangsters and writers of cops-and-robbers thrillers memorialized Gatling in one of their favorite terms for a gun—gat.

The eponymous military figures sketched in the accounts that follow are a lively, varied crew. They demonstrate that not everyone marches to the same drummer in the supposedly rigidly regimented world of the military.

James Thomas Brudenell

James Thomas Brudenell had too much too soon too easily. It was his downfall and ultimately it would become the downfall of hundreds of other Englishmen.

Son of the Earl of Cardigan, flattered and pampered from infancy, he grew to young manhood a self-centered snob, unreasonably demanding, vindictive if crossed. In his mid-twenties he requested of the authorities a suitably important post in the British army, despite his lack of training for such responsibilities. Indulged because of his aristocratic birth, he was granted command of a cavalry regiment.

The troopers were apprehensive when he arrived in 1824 to assume his command; apprehension was justified because Brudenell proved to be high-handed and erratic, meting out absurdly harsh punishment for infractions and imagined infractions of his orders. Complaints reached his superiors in such numbers that they finally relieved him of command, but shortly later he was able to secure another regiment.

Learning nothing from his experience, Brudenell was as harsh and arbitrary as before. Again, complaints mounted and there were even protests against him in parliament. They availed nothing, for his father had died, the title had passed to him, and now, as seventh Lord Cardigan, he was virtually untouchable.

Whatever else he was, Lord Cardigan was not cowardly; when England entered the Crimean War against Russia in 1854 he requested combat duty. Granted command of the Light Brigade of Cavalry, then being readied for deployment overseas, he was named a brigadier general (later to become a major general).

There was a fly in Cardigan's ointment: his brother-in-law, Lord Lucan. The two loathed each other, avoiding all contact. But the Light Brigade would be under a Crimean field headquarters commanded by Lucan who, in turn, would report to Lord Raglan, commander-in-chief of the British Expeditionary Army. Having Lucan interposed between him and Raglan was a bitter pill to swallow and Cardigan intended to ignore Lucan as much as possible.

At first, after the Light Brigade reached Crimea, it was

almost entirely an infantry war. That did not mean the cavalry's lot was a happy one. Their rations were miserable, feed for their mounts was woefully short, they slept in mud when it rained, breathed dust when it was dry. Cardigan, however, did not suffer. His yacht was anchored close by to pamper him with its luxuries.

The war was not going well for the British. The commander-in-chief, Lord Raglan, discovered that the enemy he faced was only one of his problems. Another was his French allies; led by unimaginative, indecisive generals, they were undependable. Even his superiors in London were a worry for Raglan, honoring his requisitions so slowly that he continually lacked needed supplies.

Intelligent, sensitive, and courageous, Lord Raglan deserved better than he got. As a lieutenant he had fought with Wellington at Waterloo until a sniper's bullet shattered his right arm. Walking back to the field hospital unaided, he remained conscious and silent while his arm was amputated. Shunning special favors because of his loss, he continued on active duty in increasingly more important assignments. To divert attention from his missing arm, he habitually wore a civilian frock coat with wide, loose sleeves draping down from a slanting seam commencing at the neckline.

Early on October 25, 1854, Raglan stood peering down from the heights at the mouth of a long valley stretching back from the seaport village of Balaklava. He had sent the Heavy Brigade in against the Russians holding the valley, but amid the smoke and confusion of the battle below it was not clear how it was faring.

Raglan's reserves—Cardigan's Light Brigade among

them—were being held by Lucan at the village. As usual, the two brothers-in-law avoided each other. Waiting with his troopers, Cardigan was resplendently colorful in cherry-red breeches and gleaming black boots. To ward off the chill he wore his favorite sweater, but because it was made to hang open down the front it did not hide the gilt edging on his royal blue tunic. On his head was a plumed fur shako. Raglan above and Cardigan below were sartorial contrasts—the commander-in-chief somber in his dark, loose-fitting frock coat, the Light Brigade commander dashing in peacock finery except for his open sweater.

As Raglan peered down, the smoke cleared enough to see that the Heavy Brigade was gaining the upper hand. Russian riflemen on the ridges held firm, but the enemy main body on the valley floor was falling back toward its artillery at the far end of the battlefield. Hurriedly writing orders for his reserves, Raglan dispatched them to Lucan. In his haste he did not spell out his instructions so precisely that they could not be misinterpreted. A competent officer would have understood the intent of those orders, but Lucan, not really competent, sent on to Cardigan orders that should never have been issued. Even now it was not too late if Cardigan himself were really competent and not determined to avoid Lucan—he could have caught the error and asked for correction. Instead, Cardigan mounted his horse and led his troopers at a gallop into the valley toward the artillery at the far end.

It was suicidal; artillery and rifle fire raked the Light Brigade. There was stunning, if futile, nobility in the unflinching bravery of the cavalrymen galloping into the hail of shot and shell. (Later, Tennyson would salute their courage in his poem, "The Charge of the Light Brigade.")

Miraculously untouched, Cardigan broke through behind the artillery, wheeled about, and only then realized that he was alone, that almost his entire brigade lay dead or wounded along the valley floor. Raglan on the heights above watched in horror, powerless to intervene as the Light Brigade disintegrated in a maneuver he had never intended. There was one final, incredible act in the tragedy at Balaklava. Cardigan retraced his route, riding through the valley once more—eyes forward, posture imperious—and again he emerged unscathed.

Soon afterward Lord Cardigan returned to England where, ironically under the circumstances, he was hailed as a hero. Lord Raglan, sorrowing for his fallen soldiers, was himself dead in a few months, though doctors could find no cause for death.

Oddly, both principals in the tragedy became eponymous for the distinctive garments they wore at Balaklava. From the commander-in-chief who issued the unclear order comes raglan to describe sleeves that drape from a seam slanting down from the neckline; from the man who led the Light Brigade's suicidal charge comes cardigan as a name-word for a sweater that opens down the front.

Ambrose E. Burnside

Tall, solidly built, face adorned by a luxuriant growth of whiskers that swept down from his ears to his clean-shaven chin, Ambrose E. Burnside was a fine figure of a man —imposing, dapper, and conspicuous. He sparkled in the two arenas to which he applied himself with enthusiasm: the drawing room where he charmed the ladies, and the army in which he had been commissioned following his graduation from West Point. Those who observed his maneuvers on both these fronts could not fail to note the confident adroitness with which he conducted himself.

However, after the Civil War was under way some of Burnside's magic seemed to desert him. He was as dashing as ever with the ladies but, after having risen to the rank of major general and having served with distinction in the field, his military performance began to falter. A low point came in December, 1862, when troops under his command suffered a costly defeat at the hands of a Confederate force at Fredericksburg, Virginia. President Lincoln relieved him of his post and transferred him to a lesser command. (The officer who succeeded Burnside, Major General Joseph Hooker, became eponymous by permitting a multitude of camp followers to attach themselves to his force; some were tradesmen, some washerwomen, and some prostitutes. So numerous were the latter that they came to be known as "Hooker's girls." The name took hold and still persists, shortened to hookers as a term for prostitutes.)

Accepting his rebuke with good grace, Burnside concentrated on erasing the smudge on his record. Diligently devoting himself to his diminished responsibilities, he gradually acquired a renewal of confidence in him by his superiors. Then, in 1864, he was again involved in a costly reverse in Virginia, this time in Petersburg, and once again was relieved of his command. Now there could be no hope of retrieving his military career.

After the war ended, Burnside settled in Rhode Island where he made every effort to refurbish his tarnished image. Capitalizing on his assets—the theatrical appearance, the witty conversation, the charming manners, the ability to make female hearts flutter—he overwhelmed local society. His dancing shoes turned out to be more reliable for him than his army boots had been; they carried him all the way to the governorship of the state.

In 1875, Burnside returned to the national scene when he was elected to the U.S. Senate from Rhode Island. All Washington quickly discovered that he had lost none of his enthusiasm for playing the role of the drawing room dandy. His face framed by those luxuriant whiskers that were his pride, the well-turned phrases rolling suavely from his silky-smooth tongue, he was at his gallant best in Washington's elite social circles.

However, not everyone in the nation's capital fell under Burnside's spell. His detractors were numerous and their ranks were growing, their gibes becoming more frequent and louder. They scoffed at Burnside's vanity and at his dandified ways, ridiculed his constant courting of society's upper crust, and poked fun at the two lush growths of hair sweeping down on either side of his face. The cartoonists, especially, had a field day with those side whiskers that were such tempting targets for their pens. His legion of detractors made Burnside eponymous when, playing on his name, they turned it around to "sideburns" as a term for the style of cheek whiskers he had created and on which he lavished so much attention.

Nicolas Chauvin

From the time the French Revolution erupted in 1789 until Napoleon met his ultimate defeat when Wellington vanquished him at Waterloo in 1815, France was a nation at war. During this long period of combat no French soldier took to the battlefield with more ardor than Nicolas Chauvin. Utterly devoted to Napoleon and Napoleon's cause, he was blind to any flaw in either.

A fusilier, the musket-bearing forerunner of the modern rifleman, Chauvin was always in the thick of battle, defiant and fearless. He accepted any hardship unhesitatingly, faced any danger unflinchingly for the greater glory of Napoleon and his army. Several times he was carried off the battlefield half-dead, but each time he recovered and promptly offered himself once again as a willing, even eager, sacrifice on the altar of superpatriotism. In one engagement three of his fingers were hacked off by an enemy saber; in another a bursting bomb mutilated his face so terribly that his appearance became grotesque. In all, he was wounded seventeen times.

After Napoleon's defeat Chauvin refused to accept reality, refused to acknowledge that his hero and his army had been beaten. Spouting defiance and patriotic slogans, the mutilated, bemedaled old soldier tried to rally his dejected comrades, tried to fan flames back into the ashes of defeat.

It was too late; time had passed him by. France was no longer in the mood for either military adventurism or blind superpatriotism. The press began to lampoon the scarred and battered fusilier as a fool, even a dangerous fool.

In 1831 the hit of the Paris theater season was a play about a simple-minded, exaggeratedly patriotic old soldier. The soldier on the stage, like the real-life figure on whom he was modeled, was named Chauvin. Chauvinism became a part of the French language. The word soon worked its way into other languages and gradually the original meaning became expanded. A chauvinist was no longer merely a rabid superpatriot but was now an overzealous supporter of any cause. In more recent times, sandwiched between "male" and "pig," it became especially popular as a rallying cry in the women's liberation movement. Nicolas Chauvin, blind to any cause except the one to which he dedicated his life, would be bewildered by the linguistic niche he occupies.

Lucius Licinius Lucullus

Corruption was rampant in the Rome that existed in the century before the birth of Christ. Candidates for public office bought votes, judges accepted bribes, tax collectors pocketed half of their receipts, generals sold their allegiance to the highest bidder, the subjugated peoples and lands of the far-flung empire were systematically looted of their wealth. Amid this overwhelming corruption Lucius Licinius Lucullus was a rarity. Born of a rich, aristocratic Roman family, he was a skillful and loyal general, an able and impartial administrator, and an honest man.

In 74 B.C. Lucullus led his army to the eastern provinces to quell a rebel force that had wrested a large area of Asia Minor from Roman control. His army had been undermanned and underequipped by officials who had skimmed off some of the funds intended for the expedition, but Lucullus' skillful generalship compensated for the inadequacies. The rebels slowly fell back from his assaults.

Rome should have been pleased—it was not, because as Lucullus advanced he reorganized and reformed the local administrations, making it difficult for corrupt Rome to continue squeezing the eastern provinces dry. Nor were Lucullus' soldiers pleased with their general. They had no quarrel with his military ability but they were angered by his refusal to let them pillage at will.

Egged on by emissaries from the politicians in Rome, the soldiers mutinied and Lucullus had to concentrate on putting down rebellion within his own ranks. Harassed by the enemy, compromised by an army that was now unreliable, he began withdrawing his force to Greece. In 66 B.C. Lucullus fell victim to the intrigues mounted against him when he was recalled to Rome and Pompey was named to take over his command.

If General Lucullus was bitter, he did not show it. Retiring gracefully from public life, he devoted himself to spending his great wealth in a manner that Rome had never before witnessed. He built a magnificent hilltop palace, refurbished the family estate south of Rome, bought a villa near Naples, and established a summer retreat on a coastal island. Each of his residences was luxurious, its furnishings fashioned by the most accomplished craftsmen, its walls hung with paintings by the masters, its platoons of servants highly trained. His extensive gardens were breathtakingly beautiful, planted with many species previously unknown in Italy. (The cherry tree he introduced from Asia spread to the rest of Europe and, later, to America.)

But it was the way Lucullus dined that really set Roman tongues clacking. His kitchens were staffed by masterfully innovative cooks whose performance raised food preparation to an art form. Each delectable course was an exquisite symphony orchestrated from the finest, freshest ingredients, each wine a glowing tribute to the vintner's skill. Everything was served with elegance and flair. One was in the presence of culinary greatness when one dined with Lucullus.

All Rome was consumed by envy. Everybody who was anybody set out to copy Lucullus, spending incredible sums in attempts to duplicate his life-style. They succeeded only in creating vulgar displays of tasteless ostentation. Their dinners were orgies where guests stuffed themselves into a stupor. Like Lucullus, they had the money to indulge themselves. Unlike him, they lacked the finesse and refinement. They were mass; he was class. That is why Lucullan joined the vocabulary as a synonym for sumptuous, elegant, discriminating luxury.

Cèsar du Plessis-Praslin

Count Cèsar du Plessis-Praslin knew how to squeeze the most out of the privileged life that was the envied lot of the

highborn in seventeenth-century France. He learned early
that all things were possible if one had the right family connections and capitalized on them properly. Even as a young
child he was accustomed to having his own personal staff of
servants and to ordering them about grandly. When he
"played soldier" he did it in style—with a tutor to instruct
him in military tactics. So he thought it only fitting when
he was a youth of fourteen to ask his uncle, a general in
the royal army, for a suitable military commission. Uncle
obliged. He made Cesar a colonel. Then he presented the
boy-colonel with an entire regiment of soldiers to command.

Young Plessis-Praslin loved his gift. He relished having a
regiment to order about, doted on the dash and pomp of
the parade ground. Gradually, he even succeeded in gaining sufficient understanding of the practical, workaday side
of the military, so that in time his appointment did not seem
so ludicrous. But if he was happy to *be* a colonel, he was not
for very long content to *remain* a colonel. After all, there
were higher ranks to covet and he knew exactly how to go
about getting the promotions he hungered for. So he continued exploiting his family connections, especially his kin-
ship with Cardinal Richelieu, the prelate of France and the
king's advisor on temporal as well as spiritual affairs.

Plessis-Praslin did not ignore any important officials or
members of the aristocracy who could be useful to him. He
courted them all with unflagging diligence, showering them
with gifts and entertaining them at lavish dinners where his
inventive chef created culinary surprises to delight them.
The promotions he sought came with pleasing regularity.

By the time he reached his thirties he was a lieutenant general.

Even though he had reached dizzying heights on the promotion ladder, he was not yet content. There was still higher rank to covet. So Plessis-Praslin politicked and courted and entertained. Eventually, he reached the pinnacle of military rank—he became field marshal in command of the entire royal army. But history has a way of putting matters into proper perspective. He is not remembered for the power and glory he attained as France's highest-ranking officer. Plessis-Praslin is recalled merely as the eponymous source of the praline, the sugar syrup and nut confection his chef created for the receptions Plessis-Praslin gave for those whose favor he was courting. Even his name-word, like his promotions, was not unblemished—though it retained the pronounciation of his name it altered the spelling.

Henry Shrapnel

The British army had a stroke of good fortune when it commissioned Henry Shrapnel in the Royal Artillery in 1779. It turned out that in Shrapnel the army had not only gained a keen, disciplined, and highly intelligent officer but had also found itself a genuine workaholic. Others might go off to seek their pleasures when the day's duty was done, but he remained at the barracks quite happily fussing with his regiment's artillery pieces and studying technical manuals on weaponry. The men doted on him because he so clearly knew his business and did not shrink from getting grease on his hands; fellow officers rejoiced that they could turn to him for solutions when weapons problems arose.

In time, Shrapnel developed into more than simply an authority on weaponry—he became an innovative authority able to look at guns in a fresh, imaginative way and to see possibilities that others before him had not perceived. Design improvements began to flow from him to increase performance and reliability of several of the standard artillery pieces. Promoted to captain, he was assigned to the army's Shoeburyness Experimental Establishment near London to devote full time to brainstorming improvements in weaponry.

It was at Shoeburyness in 1804 that he devised his most significant invention, a device that altered military tactics, that caused armies to adopt steel helmets for protection of troops, and that led compilers of dictionaries to add shrapnel as a new name-word. His invention was a revolutionary projectile, a spherical shell with a hollow interior containing musket balls and a small charge of black powder into which a fuse had been inserted. Until that time all artillery fired solid shot designed to do its damage by crashing into its target. This new projectile was radically different; it was not intended to hit its target. It was designed so that while it was in flight its fuse would detonate the small powder charge it carried, bursting the shell apart and flinging its cargo of musket balls outward with considerable velocity. In effect, the one big projectile thus transformed itself into dozens of hurtling miniature projectiles cutting a wide swath through troops. In the hands of a skilled gunner able to burst his shell at the right range and height, shrapnel was a devastating weapon. It became one of the most feared devices in the artilleryman's arsenal.

Consumed by a passion for technological innovation, Henry Shrapnel remained on active duty for a remarkable fifty-eight years, devoting himself to the laboratory and the proving ground and eventually reaching the rank of lieutenant general when he was seventy-six. During his long career he devised numerous other artillery developments but none so significant as his shell. A precise man accustomed to dealing with matters where exactness and accuracy were requisites, he would be annoyed that his name-word is now widely misapplied. Accounts of today's many little wars persist in attributing casualties to shrapnel, but the fact is that shrapnel no longer exists in combat, only in language. Even before World War I had ended it was already clear that shrapnel was rapidly becoming obsolete, its place taken by high-explosive shells that do not require such skillful gunners. High-explosive shells carry no on-board cargo of mini-projectiles and are not intended for air-burst; they hit their target and explode, hurtling fragments of the shell casing outward. By World War II shrapnel had all but disappeared from the arsenals of every army.

3

Thinkers and Tinkers

There is nothing flabby or juiceless about the eponymous members of the learned professions—the philosophers and scholars, the physicians, the theologians, those who think deeply about the nature of man and seek to tinker the human condition into a more pleasing state. A good case in point is John Duns, a Scot.

Philosophers and theologians had been prominent in the Duns family for several generations before John was born in 1266, and early in his life it seemed clear that he would run true to form. Even as a young child he was thoughtful, brooding, seeking answers to questions mature beyond his years. Answering those questions was not easy because he was not content with easy answers, insisting on digging to the heart of the matter and examining it minutely in logical, orderly fashion. He accepted nothing on face value, preferring to weigh it for flaws in reasoning.

After studying theology in Scotland, while still a teenager, Duns became a Franciscan friar and then went to England for further study at Oxford. Next, he enrolled at the University of Paris for an advanced degree. Along the way, in accordance with academic practice of the time, his colleagues Latinized his name to John Duns Scotus, "John Duns of Scotland." By now he was widely respected among intellectuals as an original thinker, uncompromisingly analytical in his approach to complex theological and philosophical matters. Invited to address learned bodies, he lectured in the great universities of England, France, and Germany. Increasingly, his studies and lectures were published as textbooks in many centers of learning.

But all was not smooth sailing for Duns Scotus. His brilliant, questioning mind had made him a center of controversy. The root cause was his stubborn refusal to accept conventional beliefs without evaluating them in the light of his own logic, learning, and reason. In the process, he often reached conclusions that differed—not only broadly but also in minute detail—from long-held doctrines. Scholars were aroused by his pronouncements because they altered the familiar, accepted way of looking at many complex issues. Church leaders, especially, argued over his findings.

Duns Scotus held firm, refusing to water down or compromise his views, so the academic and theological communities were forced to choose sides, some supporting his conclusions, many rejecting them. His detractors scoffed at his supporters, ridiculing them as "Dunsmen" and "Dunses" fit only to split hairs over learned matters but incapable of developing real understanding of them. In time, "Dunses" evolved into "dunces" as an abusive term for anyone of supposedly limited intelligence. Eventually—five centuries in the case of one disputed theological conclusion—the validity of most of Duns Scotus' controversial principles was established and accepted. Thus there is the great paradox of John Duns Scotus, the brilliant thinker who is memorialized by a name-word associated with ignorance.

If Duns Scotus was one-of-a-kind so, in his quite different way, was William Thompson, an Englishman born in Nottingham in 1811. From his youth onward Thompson was pulled in one direction by his body, in another by his mind. Muscular yet agile, he had the endurance, the reflexes, and the instincts of a natural athlete, as well as the zest for rough-and-tumble competition. But at the same time he was a deeply committed student of Scripture, fired with zeal to evangelize, to make believers of unbelievers and church-goers of the unchurched. Confronted by this young evangelist built like a giant, few had the temerity to turn their backs on him when he preached.

Influenced in one direction physically and in another spiritually, Thompson tried to accomodate one to the other in 1835 when he became a professional prizefighter while continuing to evangelize between matches. His religious fervor accompanied him even into the ring, for he fought under the name of Bendigo, short for Abendigo, one of the Holy Children cast into the fiery furnace by Nebuchadnezzar and delivered from the flames by an angel.

Bendigo was an awesome fighter, able to absorb punishment unflinchingly, hammering away at opponents with fists that seemed never to grow tired or slow. The battling evangelist became the darling of the ring fans and his name became known wherever boxing enthusiasts gathered.

All of the time that he was fighting his opponents Bendigo was fighting a second battle within himself, a contest between the pull of his body and the pull of his mind. His fervor to contend for souls won out over his relish for contending in the sports arena—while he was at the height of his prizefighting success he retired from the ring to devote full time to his evangelizing. A short time later he became eponymous when a city in Australia named itself Bendigo for him, and then he became eponymous for a second time when a fur cap popular toward the end of the nineteenth century was dubbed the bendigo in his honor.

Duns Scotus and Bendigo are at home among the thinkers and tinkers who follow. By and large, they are kindred spirits—all of them eponymous, all of them committed in their own way to bettering the human condition and expanding the horizons of the mind, many of them touched by controversy, many of them characterized by a streak of eccentricity.

Thomas Bowdler

Born in 1754 amid the quiet, pastoral beauty of western England's Shropshire region, Thomas Bowdler was shaped by the gentleness of his surroundings and by the gentleness of his family, long noted locally for the learned men of letters it produced. He grew to young manhood mild-mannered, soft-spoken, high-principled, and on intimate terms with the great works of literature.

When the time came to choose a career, Bowdler entered medical school, but it was a reluctant entrance undertaken only to please his father because he himself had no wish to devote himself to medicine. As he feared it would be, medical school turned out to be a mistake. He was sickened by the sight of blood and by the suffering of the ailing. However, out of regard for his father he resisted his aversion to his studies and persevered until he had earned his medical degree. As a reward, his father treated the new Dr. Bowdler to a long, leisurely tour of Europe.

Visiting Europe was another mistake. Bowdler appreciated the art, the music, the cathedrals, and palaces that the Continent had to offer. It was the people that upset him. The bawdiness and lax morality that he glimpsed all around him conflicted disturbingly with his rigid view of what was proper. So the European tour was a two-edged sword that cut deeply. On one hand he welcomed the delay in establishing his medical practice; on the other he was distressed by the moral lapses he witnessed. In the end he was not sorry when the time came to return home.

Dr. Bowdler opened his practice in London. He tried to console himself with the thought that he was striving to eliminate the suffering of his patients, but it did little to ease the acute discomfort he experienced among them. Their miseries became his miseries. His only real relief came when he opened his books and lost himself in the world of literature.

In 1800, having come into a considerable inheritance,

Bowdler was in a position to end his unwanted role as a doctor. Feeling that an oppressive weight was lifting from him, he abandoned London and medicine, settling on the quiet Isle of Wight in the English Channel. The isolation of his new home pleased him, insulating him from the distress he had experienced to the north among London's ailing and to the south among Europe's bawdy dissipators. Here he was free to devote himself entirely to his beloved books.

One of Bowdler's favorite authors was William Shakespeare. He savored the richness of Shakespeare's works, the graceful phrases and glowing imagery of his sonnets, the verve of his comedies, the finely drawn characters, dramatic sweep and splendid prose of his plays. However, despite the magnificence of his work, Shakespeare had one drawback that disturbed Bowdler greatly. Bowdler was convinced that Shakespeare often wrote of human weakness and folly with such frankness that innocent, virtuous readers—especially female readers—were exposed to passages that could only shock and offend them. The solution seemed obvious to Bowdler—he would render Shakespeare suitable for even the most delicate and virtuous of ladies by removing from the author's writings any portions that might be an affront to their dignity, sensitivity, and delicacy.

Undertaking his mission with enthusiasm, Dr. Bowdler commenced revising Shakespeare's works, removing words that seemed to him to be too earthy, toning down dialogue that was too suggestive, snipping away scenes that were too explicit. It was a long, arduous task but by 1818 he had completed his ten-volume *Family Shakespeare*. When it was published there was a loud chorus of outraged complaint over his literary tinkering. Bowdler, surprised because he was condemned instead of hailed for cleaning up the Bard of Avon's act, stoutly defended his purging of what he termed "obscenity." Then, having sanitized Shakespeare, he set out to render the same service for Edward Gibbon. Before he died in 1825 he had produced an expurgated version of Gibbon's monumental *The History of the Decline and Fall of the Roman Empire.* His zeal as a self-appointed censor had only one lasting result. It made bowdlerizing a name-word for prudish expurgation of a literary work.

Sylvester Graham

As a solemn child in his native Connecticut, Sylvester Graham was not very popular with other boys. It wasn't only because he was so earnest and grave, never joining in their fun, but also because he argued with them insistently that it was wrong to play pranks. The fact is that Graham was a born uplifter, driven by an inner urge to discourage those around him from giving in to the weaknesses of the flesh. Nobody was surprised when, after graduating from Amherst College, he entered a seminary and then was ordained a Presbyterian minister.

For a while Reverend Graham was quite content with his ministry. A vigilant shepherd of his little flock, he was tireless in his efforts to strengthen their faith, industrious in undertaking to repair cracks in their moral armor, and eloquent in his pulpit sermons. Gradually, however, he began to feel the need to pursue his uplifting with a wider audience than just his small congregation. At that time—the mid-1850s—the movement to stamp out "Demon Rum" was commencing to stir, especially in the central part of the country, and Graham saw in it a vehicle through which he could accomplish good works on behalf of a larger constituency. He moved from the pulpit to the temperance lecture circuit, ranging over a wide area to deliver his messages condemning strong drink.

Over the months, as he tried to enlist his audiences into the battle against alcohol, Graham thought deeply about his subject, analyzing the nature of alcoholism and developing a theory about what it was that greased the slide into the bottle. He became convinced that there was a cause-and-effect link between food and drink. The way people ate, he came to believe, influenced the way they drank. Change your eating habits, he urged listeners, and you break the chains of the bottle. He appealed to them to abandon all meats, fish, and "unnatural" foods and instead to consume vegetables and fruits accompanied by sips of cold water.

Others before him had advocated vegetarianism, though never as an antidote to alcoholism. His diet, however, added a new wrinkle of his own invention: a cracker to be baked of whole grain, unsifted wheat flour, and then to be set aside until it had become brittle. After the crackers were within hailing distance of staleness they were to be eaten in small bites that were to be chewed slowly and thoroughly before being swallowed. Many ridiculed his dietary program and his crackers, but Graham, a forceful and convincing speaker, managed to win over a fair share of converts.

To amplify the reach of his message, Graham wrote several books extolling his ideas as a cure for alcoholism and as a pathway to good health. A number of bakeries added his crackers to their offerings, although it is not clear whether they believed the benefit would accrue to their customers at the dinner table or to themselves at the cash drawer. In addition, a sprinkling of health spas began featuring his menus, including his crackers. For a few years Graham's diet enjoyed a certain measure of popularity, attracting a handful of influential adherents like Horace Greeley, editor of the *New York Tribune.* But old habits die hard and both meat and alcohol were formidable opponents; Graham could not deal them a knockout blow. However, all was not lost—graham crackers lingered on to gain a solid foothold and to emerge as a grocery shelf staple, and years later modern nutritionists would confirm that the eponymous crusader was on the right track when he tried tinkering with the diet to introduce graham crackers and natural foods into it.

Graham's star had hardly waned when a new voice was raised to plead for change in dietary customs. It belonged to an English physician, James Henry Salisbury. His message was the exact opposite of Graham's in at least one respect. Where the Reverend Sylvester Graham had been adamantly opposed to meat, Dr. Salisbury championed it earnestly in the form of chopped beef patties. To enhance the benefits of his patties he had devised a recipe for them that incorporated milk, eggs, and bread crumbs into the meat mixture. Dubbed "Salisbury steak," the patties gained a wide following and worked their way into both cookbooks and dictionaries. But like many zealots, Salisbury did not know where to draw the line. He urged all who would heed him to go all-out in consecrating their digestive tracts to Salisbury steaks—for breakfast, for lunch, and for dinner. One can only assume he would rejoice to see today's vast, neon-lit, international army of hamburger restaurants, even though their beef lacks the added nutritive value of his Salisbury steak.

Joseph Ignace Guillotin

An eminent physician in Paris in the years just before the French Revolution, Joseph Ignace Guillotin was also a man of deep social conscience, concerned not only with the quality of the public's health care but also with the quality of its life generally. So when Louis XVI, hoping to quiet the revolutionary spirit starting to stir in France, convened a national legislature in 1789 it seemed fitting that Dr. Guillotin was elected a member to represent the public interest. As a legislator he sought several reforms, chief among them an improvement in the criminal justice system. To this end, he proposed several changes in the existing penal code, especially a change in the matter of capital punishment.

Dr. Guillotin did not argue that, where warranted by the offense, the death penalty should not be imposed; however, he protested the manner in which executions were performed. Peasants sentenced to death were hanged, sometimes writhing for long moments of agony as the noose accomplished its work. Condemned noblemen were beheaded and often they, too, endured agony when the executioner's aim was off its mark and he botched the job. Guillotin proposed that both hangman and swordsman be replaced by a uniform, more effective method of execution that would be instantaneous and mistake-proof and would erase distinction between peasant and nobleman. This could be done, he told the Assembly, by introducing a decapitating machine that would snuff out life humanely with one swift, flawless blow. He described how the machine would work: a sharp blade suspended between guide rails above the condemned man's neck would, when released by the executioner, plunge unerringly to shear off the head. The Assembly instructed the Academy of Medicine to study the proposal.

For two years the Academy debated the merits of mechanical decapitation and the specifics of a suitable design. At the end of that period the Academy's secretary, Dr. Antoine Louis, reported to the Assembly that such a machine was feasible and would indeed be humane and efficient. He accompanied the report with detailed design specifications he himself had worked out. The legislators adopted both the report and the design, decreeing that henceforth all sentences of death would be carried out by mechanical beheading. A German carpenter, Tobias Schmidt, was granted the contract to construct the machine, which was immediately dubbed the Louisette for Dr. Louis.

With typical Germanic thoroughness, Schmidt did a splendid job on the Louisette, thoughtfully including a leather bag to catch the head neatly as it was severed. The machine was installed in a public square in Paris and received its first customer, a convicted felon, on April 22,

1792. Thereafter it was in constant use, a consequence of the intensifying upheavals and disorders of that period.

Only one month after the machine began separating Frenchmen from their heads, it became somewhat inappropriate to continue calling it the Louisette, since Dr. Louis, its designer, had fallen afoul of the regime and on May 20 was decapitated by his own machine. Anyway, many people had all along referred to it as a guillotine, to honor the man who first proposed it, and now everyone adopted that name.

More than anything else, the guillotine became the symbol of that bloody era that came to be known as France's Reign of Terror. Thus, Dr. Joseph Ignace Guillotin, whose only objective had been to introduce a humane measure, became eponymous for a device symbolizing inhumanity, a device he did not design and did not construct. He did not even originate the idea—over the centuries decapitating machines had been used in a few other places and it was his knowledge of this that had led him to propose adoption of such a device by France.

Franz Anton Mesmer

Medicine in the mid-eighteenth century was emerging from the Dark Ages, shaking loose from the clutches of the quacks, the compounders of magic remedies for every human ailment, the barbers who did double-duty as surgeons and in the process proved only that their skill lay in cutting hair, not bodies. It was a time of transition for medicine into a science based on fact instead of myth and superstition. The microscope had been improved into a more sensitive tool and the clinical thermometer had been developed. Research into anatomy and physiology had strengthened medical knowledge. The mysteries of digestion were beginning to be solved and the role of proper hygiene to be understood.

But amid the stirrings of genuine progress in medical science, quackery and superstition continued to thrive. Bleeding patients to draw off "bad" blood was still widespread; in France alone in that period the lives of some 40,000 patients leaked away each year in the streams of blood drained from them. In England, Parliament paid Joanna Stevens 5,000 pounds for her secret gallstone remedy; what the legislators got was a recipe for a brew of snails, soap, eggshells, and seed whose only benefit was to enrich Joanna at the expense of the British taxpayer.

It was against this background that Franz Anton Mesmer obtained his medical degree in Vienna in 1766. The thirty-three-year-old Austrian, already holding degrees in law and philosophy, had a restlessly inquisitive mind coupled with an original way of seeing intellectual problems. Never was this more evident than in the thesis he submitted as the final step in obtaining his medical degree—he asserted that cures could be effected by manipulating "magnetic waves" in conjunction with astrological influences. The university did not judge the validity of this surprising thesis, simply accepting it on the basis of originality.

Setting up offices in Vienna, Mesmer began putting his theory into practice, treating patients by rubbing magnets over the parts of their bodies that ailed them. Later he discarded his magnets because, he claimed, he had discovered that he possessed the power to create healing magnetic waves merely by touching patients with his hands. So the ill came, paid their fees, and were stroked. In 1778 the Austrian authorities, finally rendering a judgment on Mesmer, declared him a fraud and gave him two days to leave the country. He headed for France.

Paris proved to be hospitable. Mesmer started by writing a book trumpeting praises for his discovery of "animal magnetism" as a cure-all; then, having set the stage, he opened an office and got down to business. His treatment was now more elaborate than in Vienna. In one phase he placed his hand on his patients while they held a "magnetic" tray fitted with iron studs and containing a foul-smelling mixture of chemicals. In another, he "mesmerized" his willing subjects by placing his face close to theirs and staring fixedly into their eyes until they were drowsy and passive; having produced a state of submissiveness in them, he then told them compellingly that they felt better.

Mesmer created a sensation. Patients—including the rich, the titled, and the educated—flocked to him to be magnetized and mesmerized. One was the Marquis de Lafayette, fresh from his triumphs in America. Another was the Duchess de Bourbon. Pastor Johann Kaspar Lavater, Switzerland's most noted churchman, prayed for his ill wife's recovery but played safe by following Mesmer's instructions for mesmerizing her to good health. In only one year Dr. Mesmer was a millionaire.

In 1785 the French Academy of Sciences appointed a

commission to investigate Mesmer. (One commission member was Dr. Guillotin; another was Benjamin Franklin, then serving in Paris as agent of the new United States government.) Striving to be impartial, the commission conceded that Mesmer appeared to have helped some patients with only minor ailments but it discredited the portions of his treatment related to magnetism. Acting on the report, the government denounced Mesmer as a charlatan, expropriated his fortune, and banished him from France. He went to Switzerland.

The urge to resume his unconventional treatment was still strong in Mesmer but, having been officially labeled a quack in two different countries and having been expelled from both, in Switzerland he was in no position to return to his old ways. Yet, it would be unjust to dismiss him as merely a fraud because that would imply that he schemed to deceive his patients. The fact is that he was quite serious about his work, convinced that there was merit in what he had been doing, that it had a fundamental validity he did not quite understand.

Dr. Mesmer lived out his days quietly in Switzerland, now and then ministering to patients by conventional means, dying there in 1815 at the age of eighty-two. Some years later a British doctor, James Braid, made a thorough study of Mesmer's work. He found no value in much of it but concluded there was potential benefit in mesmerization, for which he coined a new term: hypnotism. Today, mesmerization—or hypnotism—is an accepted medical tool, but it is only one among many available to medical science. It is not, as its eponymous pioneer seemed so clearly to believe, a cure for all ailments. Modern medical textbooks list mesmero-mania as a mental disorder defined as unreasonable, obsessive devotion to mesmerization.

Jean Nicot

Jean Nicot was neither unusually conceited nor driven by overwhelming ambition. However, he did hope that in some modest way he might leave behind something worthwhile to be remembered by when his time on earth was ended. Son of a minor French official, he was a bookish sort with academic instincts, so he thought he had hit on the ideal legacy to leave for posterity when he began in his mid-twenties to compile a dictionary of the French language. In 1594, the sixty-fourth and final year of his life, he completed his massive undertaking to produce the world's first French dictionary. But it is not for that accomplishment that he is best remembered. Instead, it is for a simple, well-meaning act of his years earlier in which he unwittingly set in motion a major conflict that still persists.

His bright intellect and unimpeachable integrity having come to the attention of the royal court, Nicot was dispatched to Lisbon in 1559 on a confidential mission to King Sebastian I of Portugal. Conscientious in serving French interests, Nicot, on learning that a Portuguese expedition to America had lately returned with a strange New World plant, obtained some of the seeds and sent them to Paris. Intrigued by the unknown, agriculturalists attached to the French court sowed the seeds, growing Europe's first crop of the strange American plant. In honor of Jean Nicot, they assigned to it the scientific name of *Nicotiana.* By the time, years later, that other scientists analyzing the plant discovered in it a poisonous alkaloid—which they called *nicotine*—the plant had already become a center of mounting controversy.

Many Europeans had adopted the custom of inhaling the smoke of burning nicotiana leaves in the fashion of the American Indian smoking his pipe. Even more widespread was the custom of sniffing a pinch of the powdered leaves of nicotiana, or tobacco as the Spanish persisted in calling it. It was all the rage, especially among the upper classes; few people seemed to feel themselves fully dressed unless they carried with them their little boxes of tobacco.

Many leaders of the Catholic Church attacked this addiction to the plant on the grounds that its use on Holy Days constituted a breaking of obligations for fasting, and one Pope excommunicated those who persisted in smoking or sniffing during fast times. The Swiss Parliament went so far as to adopt legislation establishing tobacco use as a cardinal sin, while the Czar of Russia threatened to have the noses cut off of confirmed sniffers. On the other hand, ministers of finance throughout Europe regarded with satisfaction this public demand for tobacco because they had found that the imposition of a tax on the leaves had become a pleasing new source of income for their treasuries. Supporting them enthusiastically were merchants keen for the profit in catering to the needs of the smokers and sniffers. Eventually the religious aspects of the issue dwindled away and punitive measures against users were abandoned. Then the flames of controversy were fanned anew when doctors in many countries, especially the United States, began warning of health hazards associated with absorption of nicotine into the body. With the passage of time the flames have waxed hotter.

So scholarly Jean Nicot, who wished to leave society a worthwhile legacy and devoted most of his life to compiling an entire book of words for posterity, achieved linguistic fame with a single, inflammatory name-word that did not even appear in the dictionary he fashioned.

William Archibald Spooner

To say that William Archibald Spooner was born in London is simply to acknowledge a biographical fact. In a less literal but more significant sense, he was really born when he arrived at Oxford University's New College as a student in 1862. It was there in those academic surroundings that he came alive as a devoted admirer of scholarship and of students. After receiving his undergraduate degree, Spooner remained on at New College, obtaining an appointment as a teaching fellow.

When he was not amid his students, Spooner was amid his cherished books, delving deeply into the two fields that interested him most: theology and history. Developing an intimate appreciation of each field, he succeeded in linking them by writing learned works tracing the historical growth of religious influences and institutions. In the meantime, he became ordained into the priesthood of the Church of England. His commitment to the cloth was profound but it did not interfere with his commitment to the campus. He regarded the college as his proper parish, so he assumed the functions of chaplain of the institution in addition to his academic role on the staff. Then he and the college became even more closely intertwined when he was elevated to the post of dean of students.

Dean Spooner was beloved by students and faculty alike. They doted on him for all of the expectable reasons—his scholarship, his kind, generous spirit, his gentle humor and warmth—and also for an unusual reason, his metathesis. Metathesis is a speech condition in which the speaker involuntarily sometimes transposes initial sounds of words so that, as once happened to Spooner, his metathesized attempt to say "a crushing blow" comes out "a blushing crow."

Whenever Spooner was to address a group—and as both dean and chaplain he had few gaps in his speaking schedule—he faced standing-room-only audiences, everyone anticipating a memorable spoonerism. This exerted psychological pressure on him that increased his verbal slips, so that his listeners were seldom disappointed. On one occasion "our dear old queen" came out as "our queer old dean" and on another "a half-formed wish" became "a half-warmed fish." The fame of spoonerisms spread far beyond Oxford and many inventive individuals began manufacturing their own counterfeits of the genuine article, so that often it is impossible to distinguish the real from the impostor.

There was permanence to the love affair between Dean Spooner and New College. It did not languish even when old age finally forced him to relinquish an active role in campus affairs. He simply strolled over from his nearby home, as often as the weather and his advancing years permitted, to be among the students and the books that nourished him and to deliver an occasional address spiced with such amusing slips as his transformation of "conquering kings" into "kinkering congs." Dean Spooner died at Oxford in 1930, leaving behind a name-word that evokes smiles.

4

Life Among the Politicians

Aristotle observed more than 2,000 years ago that "Man is a political animal." Aristotle was right and nothing has changed in all the intervening centuries. Politics is the lubricant of the human community. Sometimes the politicians apply the lubricant skillfully, sometimes clumsily, sometimes in measured amounts, and sometimes excessively. But however they do it, they do it ceaselessly. Because they are so many and so active, politicians have inspired a substantial number of name-words. Reflecting the character of the figures from whom they are derived, they are among the most colorful and lively of our words.

As a politician, Niccolò Machiavelli is in a class by himself. Born into a prominent fifteenth-century Italian family in Florence, he got his political feet wet as a young administrative aide in the government of the Florentine city-state. Machiavelli never got out of the water. He became by turn

Florence's ambassador to France, to the Vatican, and to Germany, and its minister of defense.

An intimate observer of the political trickery practiced by the powerful Borgia and de Medici families, he knew most of the important European public figures of his time and studied them closely. Noting everything and forgetting nothing, he became a politician's politician, frequently called on by European leaders for advice and counsel. Machiavelli was a Niagara of ideas, gushing forth fresh concepts in a constant outpouring. He set down many of his views in books that are among the most influential, most quoted, and most controversial to come from the pen of a politician.

In one of his books, *Discourses,* he propounded the first theories to envision establishment of a republican form of government. In another, *On the Art of War,* he developed the concept that military problems cannot be solved in isolation from political factors. But his major work, *The Prince,* is the one that captured most attention and provoked most arguments.

After the republican principles he put forth in his *Discourses, The Prince* is a surprise. In it Machiavelli explains his formula for taking and holding power, a formula many interpret as urging any means, however oppressive, to gain power. (One of his rules—"Princes should delegate to others the enactment of unpopular measures"—is practiced widely today under the heading of "passing the buck.") Some insist he was simply being satirical in justifying any force or deceit as a legitimate means of gaining a desired political end. Others believe Machiavelli was not actually applauding treachery but was only making a realistic appraisal of the way politics operate. In any event, much of what he outlined in the book is practiced today in what the world has come to know as "power politics." Whatever the truth of his intentions in *The Prince*, the book has made Machiavellian a name-word for cunning and deceitful.

One who in this century was frequently accused of playing power politics was Theodore Roosevelt, twenty-sixth president of the United States. Critics supported their accusation by citing his "gunboat diplomacy" and his "speak softly but carry a big stick" policy. Supporters portrayed him as a "people's president," citing his regulation of free-wheeling "big business," his efforts to safeguard consumers' interests, and his initiation of measures to conserve natural resources and protect the environment. But when he became eponymous it was not for the policies his critics condemned nor for those his boosters praised. Teddy Roosevelt became eponymous because a group of Southern politicians outsmarted themselves when they invited him on a bear hunt in Mississippi.

Leaving nothing to chance, his hosts tied a captured bear cub to a tree and then led the president to it for the kill. Angered by this lack of sportsmanship, Roosevelt ordered the bear freed and stalked off the field without firing a shot. A Washington newspaper printed a cartoon depicting the incident, other newspapers reprinted it, and the whole nation learned how Teddy Roosevelt saved the helpless animal from slaughter. To cash in on the publicity, a manufacturer rushed into production with a cuddly little toy cub. Since then, generations of children around the world have had their teddy bears.

There is a Biblical injunction that "Wide is the gate, and broad is the way, that leadeth to destruction." Teddy Roosevelt and Niccolò Machiavelli—one eponymous for a trifling incident, the other for a matter of overwhelming significance—demonstrate that wide is the gate, and broad is the way, that leadeth politicians to eponymy.

Charles Cunningham Boycott

The crops in Ireland had been poor for several years but in 1880 the bottom fell out. The fields yielded nothing and all Ireland suffered. For the luckless farmers, however, there was a special note of tragedy.

Almost all of the country's tillable acreage was concentrated in the hands of wealthy, powerful absentee owners back in England. Managers representing the absentees administered the estates, employing field hands to cultivate part of the holdings but renting out the major portion to local tenant farmers. In the best of times the tenants had been hard-pressed to meet their high monthly rents, and these were the worst of times. Unmoved by the plight of the farmers, the absentee landlords ordered their estate managers to evict those who fell behind in their payments. Now, without an 1880 harvest to carry them over, enormous numbers of tenants faced eviction.

Irish political leaders raised their voices in angry protest over the impending mass evictions. The most vocal of them, and the most prominent, was Charles Stewart Parnell. An ardent nationalist, he had formed the Irish National Land League to press Ireland's political masters in the British Parliament for adoption of land-reform legislation easing the burden of the landless tenant farmers. With the situation having reached crisis stage, Parnell now urged tenants to reject the high rent scales imposed on them and to unilaterally assume a lower, more reasonable level of payments. Beyond that, he urged that if a landlord refused the lower rent or attempted to evict a tenant, all workers employed by him should walk off their jobs and isolate him "as if he were a leper." It was in a fiery speech to a large assembly of farmers in County Mayo that Parnell made his militant proposals. Within days they bore their first fruit.

County Mayo's largest absentee owner, the Earl of Erne, was not a man to be trifled with and the estate manager he had sent out from England, an ex-army captain named Charles Cunningham Boycott, was cut from the same mold. So when the tenants on the Erne property offered reduced payments, Boycott refused to accept them and ordered them off the land. Fired up by Parnell, the people of County Mayo closed ranks solidly against Boycott, isolating him even more rigidly than the militant political leader had envisaged.

Everyone on the Erne estate walked off the job—field hands, stable workers, house servants, foremen—some stealing back at night to tear down fences and to damage farm equipment. Local merchants refused to sell any supplies to Boycott. The blacksmith would not shoe his horses, the veterinarian would not treat his animals, the laundress would not wash his linens, the postman would not deliver his mail.

When Boycott ventured into town he was jeered and threatened. The situation became so tense that he was forced to flee to England.

Parnell's tactics succeeded. The wall of total isolation proved to be a potent weapon, accomplishing what years of pleading had failed to achieve—Britain passed the long-sought land-reform legislation. The lesson of County Mayo was not lost on the rest of the world. The estate manager who was the political pawn in the first test of the new technique became the eponymous source of boycott as a name-word and as a practice that quickly became international.

Elbridge Gerry

There has never been another fishmonger quite like El-bridge Gerry. He entered the family codfish-trading company in Marblehead, Massachusetts, following graduation from Harvard in 1763; he had been exposed to the ferment of political philosophies bubbling on the Harvard campus and he never got over it. He did his duty by the fish but continued his active involvement in politics and in 1772 was named to represent Marblehead in the Massachusetts General Court.

At Court sessions Gerry came under the wing of firebrand Samuel Adams, absorbing from him a deep resolve to seek American independence. Elected to the Continental Congress in January, 1776, Gerry campaigned hard in that body for a complete break with England. He felt a great surge of satisfaction and pride when the legislators ultimately approved the Declaration of Independence without dissent.

Now that the die was cast, Gerry turned his fishmongering into a national asset. Throughout the Revolution he used his fish-exporting channels and his overseas business contacts to procure foreign supplies sorely needed by Washington's army.

After the American cause prevailed, Gerry was named to the convention assembled to write the Constitution for the new republic, but refused to sign that document when that body declined to include his wording in it. Despite this, he was elected to the first U.S. Congress in 1789 and reelected to the second. These were stormy sessions, Gerry contributing to the storms by demanding, unsuccessfully, that the president be denied a cabinet to advise him, on grounds that counselling the president was a function of Congress.

The next political turmoil involving Gerry occurred in 1797 when a Franco-American dispute was worsening dangerously. President John Adams named him to a three-man commission to go to Paris to negotiate a settlement. Talleyrand, the French foreign minister, refused to see the commission, hinting that bribes and loans to France could persuade him to change his mind. Outraged, two of the members left but the third, Gerry—confident he could maneuver the situation to the advantage of the United States—remained. Angered that Gerry would submit to such demeaning circumstances, Adams ordered him home, where he found himself snubbed by many former friends.

Nevertheless, politics had become his way of life and he continued active in the affairs of the Jeffersonian Party.

In 1810 Gerry won the governorship of Massachusetts and became involved in new controversy by discharging all Federalists holding posts in the state administration. Adding fuel to the fire, he signed into law in 1812 a bill altering boundaries of state voting districts in a way that minimized ballot box strength of the Federalists while maximizing that of the Jeffersonians. "Dirty politics!" cried the Federalists but Gerry shrugged it off.

Shortly after Gerry rigged the ballot box, Gilbert Stuart, the eminent artist, visited a newspaper editor who showed him a map of newly carved-up Essex County. With his artist's eye, Stuart could perceive an animal's form in the county's grotesquely altered shape. Drawing a few lines on the map to add a head, wings, and claws, Stuart exclaimed, "There, that will do for a salamander." "Call it a gerrymander," the editor replied.

Despite manipulating voting districts to tilt ballots in his favor, Gerry lost his race for reelection to the governorship. The Jeffersonians immediately placed him on their national ticket as their vice presidential candidate. This time he won, but after only one year in office he died at age seventy. Elbridge Gerry had come far since his days as a fishmonger. If along the way he had engaged in shoddy politics, he had also rendered the nation signal services. The years have drawn a veil of forgetfulness over this complex man, in effect reducing his epitaph to a single word: gerrymandering. It is a word, and a practice, that persists, leading later politicians to create such gerrymandered voting districts as today's "Horseshoe" district of New York, "Monkey Wrench" district of Iowa, and "Dumbbell" district of Pennsylvania.

William Lynch

The United States was only a dozen years past the Revolution that created it when historians began trying to trace the roots of a word that was becoming increasingly common in the new nation: lynching—the illegal execution, usually by hanging, of an individual thought to be guilty of a crime. They believed the word had originated in Virginia, so they knew where to concentrate their search. The trail led them to Bedford County in the southwestern part of the state and to Charles Lynch, brother of the founder of the city of Lynchburg.

Charles Lynch had been a member of the Virginia House of Burgesses, a militia colonel, and a magistrate of the Bedford County Court at the time the Revolution began. During the war he had remained in Bedford keeping his court functioning. Under Virginia law of that time, county courts were empowered to try only those accused of minor offenses, while those charged with major crimes had to be taken to the court in Williamsburg to stand trial. But Bedford lay 200 miles to the west of Williamsburg and once the war began much of the territory between the two was controlled by the British or by Tories loyal to the British. Since it was now too dangerous to transport the accused to Williamsburg, Lynch solved the problem by trying all who were brought before him, whether or not he had legal jurisdiction over their alleged offenses.

After the Revolution some of those who had been tried under "Lynch's law" complained to state authorities that their trials had been illegal. The legislature conducted an investigation into the matter, concluding that Colonel Lynch's actions were justified by "the imminence of the danger."

Historians accepted all of this as a reasonable explanation of how lynching was created as a name-word, although some wondered why the term should mean illegal executions when Lynch had passed no death sentences. Then along came Edgar Allan Poe to shed fresh light on the matter.

In a newspaper article he wrote in 1836, Poe pointed the finger at another Virginian whose background was remarkably similar to that of the man from Bedford County. William Lynch, unrelated to Charles though both shared the same surname, lived in Pittsylvania, the county adjoining Bedford. Like Charles, he was active in local politics and was a militia colonel. Toward the end of the Revolution, William Lynch and his neighbors were being harassed by an outlaw band that roamed Pittsylvania, looting and evading capture by local authorities. Provoked beyond endurance, Lynch took it upon himself to organize a number of Pittsylvanians into an extra-legal group to enforce the law and to punish those who broke it. Poe included in his article the document that William Lynch drew up on September 22, 1780, to bring his vigilante group into existence. In it Lynch declared that "we will forthwith embody ourselves" to apprehend these "vile miscreants" and "we will inflict such corporeal punishment . . . as to us shall seem adequate to the crime committed."

Another who pointed the finger at William of Pittsylvania rather than Charles of Bedford as the eponymous source of lynching is Andrew Elliot, who came to know the Pittsylvanian in 1811 after he had moved from Virginia to South Carolina. Recounting conversations they held, Elliot wrote in his diary that William Lynch had conceded that some of the "vile miscreants" they caught were hanged.

William Lynch, no longer active as a self-appointed law enforcer, lived out his days quietly and died in South Carolina in 1820. But the damage had been done—lynching had become established as a name-word and as a corruption of the law. And the weight of evidence seems clearly to establish the man from Pittsylvania as both the eponym and the corrupter.

Joel Robert Poinsett

Monied and socially prominent, the Poinsetts of Charleston, South Carolina, were accustomed to doing things in the grand manner, so they were running true to form when they sent young Joel Robert Poinsett to England to study medicine *and* law. For several years he pursued his twin studies while at the same time maintaining a lively interest in politics. He imagined himself one day turning from scalpels and law briefs to devote full attention to affairs of government. He was forced to turn from them sooner than anticipated when failing health caused him to abandon England and return home. After a long convalescence he was again ready to resume an active life and now he became engaged directly in politics.

In 1810 President Madison asked Poinsett to undertake a delicate mission to South America. Several countries in the southern continent were embroiled in struggles for independence and Madison wanted an assessment of their chances of success. The reports Poinsett sent back proved him an energetic, penetrating observer able to see beyond the slogans, the bluster, and the impractical dreams. His mission completed, he returned to South Carolina where he won a seat in the state legislature in 1815. Six years later he was elected to the U.S. House of Representatives.

Though involved in national affairs, Poinsett followed developments south of the border with lively interest, so he was pleased in 1825 to be named first United States minister to the new Mexican republic. Assuming his post, he found the country fragmented by dissension.

Poinsett's first task was organizing the U.S. mission; once that was accomplished he tried to sort out the turbulent Mexican situation. Not content simply to examine the government's policies and intentions, he traveled throughout Mexico contacting dissidents to hear their complaints and evaluate their plans. All of this convinced him the regime in power was inept and unresponsive to the needs and aspirations of most of its citizens. Concluding that the dissidents were closer to the mark, he strengthened his ties to them, offering advice and encouragement. Angered by his meddling, Mexico complained to Washington. When that got no results, it demanded Poinsett's recall. Washington ordered him home in 1829.

Returning to South Carolina, Poinsett was not yet ready to abandon politics. However, he was now fifty and his health was again troublesome, so he assumed the role of an elder statesman, giving counsel when asked but leaving the battles to others to wage. (He relented in 1837 to accept a four-year stint as secretary of war, during which he opposed states' righters seeking veto power over all Federal actions.)

In Charleston, Poinsett was caught up in an interest that had been sparked during his travels around Mexico where he had come across a strange, colorful native plant that fascinated him. When ordered back to the United States, he took specimens of it with him. Now, patiently and carefully, he propagated them, gradually breeding into them tolerance for the more northern climate. From his efforts emerged the plant that has become the floral symbol of Christmas and that takes its name from him: the poinsettia.

There is an odd parallel between Poinsett and a fellow Charlestonian of a half-century earlier, Alexander Garden. Like Poinsett, Garden studied medicine in England and then returned to Charleston to become active in politics and botany. He was opposed to American independence and when the Revolution succeeded, Garden left for permanent residence in England. To honor him for his loyal support of the British and his activity as a noted amateur botanist, The Royal Society named a flowering shrub for him—the gardenia.

Étienne de Silhouette

The worst of the winter of 1759 was behind France, but Frenchmen could not look forward to a spring that would bring them cheer. Although the seasons would change, the prospects would remain bleak and chilly, for this was now the third year of the nation's bitter, costly, steadily worsening Seven Years' War. The country—its politics in disarray, its economy in shambles, its treasury drained—teetered on the brink of bankruptcy.

Recognizing that the nation desperately needed a strong-willed, resourceful, fiscal innovator to reshape its failing economic policies, the Marquise de Pompadour—the power behind the French throne—cast about for such an individual. She found him in Étienne de Silhouette, a fifty-year-old economist who had published penetrating and shrewd studies of the French situation. At her urging, King Louis XV appointed him Controller General of Finance.

Silhouette knew he faced two problems that had to be addressed simultaneously: how to increase the country's revenues, and how to reduce its expenditures. He was realist enough to recognize that he would be threading his way through a political minefield, that every fiscal reform he proposed would anger the group that felt its pinch most.

Silhouette had the courage of his convictions. He buckled down immediately to attacking the chaotic economic situation in ways that France had not previously known.

To start with, Silhouette eliminated the traditional right of tax collectors to retain for themselves a significant portion of their collections, and he made everyone liable to taxation, including the nobility and government officials who were previously exempt. He called for an immediate reduction in state pensions, a mandatory turn-in of silver in exchange for paper currency, and an end to public funding of the king's considerable gambling losses. He proposed that the heavy land tax, until then applicable only to farmers, now be extended to the estates of the nobility and the Church.

All of this was exceedingly strong medicine but Silhouette busily compounded more bitter pills for France to swallow—a series of brand-new taxes that included a levy against those with servants and carriages and one against bachelors, a sales tax on all consumer goods, and a special tax on luxury goods.

Sparing no one, the radical program angered everyone. Because the French are usually never so grievously wounded as when pricked in the pocketbook, howls of protest went up on all sides. Especially outraged were the nobility and the wealthy, since they stood to lose the most. They complained angrily that if the drastic measures were enforced they would be sucked dry, becoming empty figures "silhouetted" into mere shadows of themselves. Political considerations won out over fiscal reform—Étienne de

Silhouette was dismissed from office and his program was abandoned. Though he had been Controller General for only eight months, he is remembered in the enduring name-word for a shadowed outline, a silhouette.

Martin Van Buren

In his time Martin Van Buren was a political power to be reckoned with, although today he rates only a meager foot-note in the history of the nation. It is, in its way, a curious twist of irony because his name—at least his nickname—has become what is probably the most used expression in the English language. It has also migrated around the world to become popular internationally.

Born in 1782 in Kinderhook, a rural community in up-state New York, Van Buren helped out with the family ploughing and planting but his heart was not really in it. What exerted a magnetic pull on him early in life was the give-and-take and excitement of politics. It was an attraction that never diminished for him.

Then as now, the most common stepping-stone to public office was the practice of law, so Van Buren "read law" with a local attorney and in 1803 was admitted to the bar. For the next ten years he patiently carved out a position of prominence in county affairs, then he ran for a seat in the New York legislature and won by a comfortable margin. A skillful organizer, in his new power-base in Albany he forged a tight-knit group of statehouse leaders that became the hub around which the state's politics revolved. With the leverage of this influential group, in 1821 he was able to vault into national prominence as U.S. senator from New York. Seven years later Van Buren returned to Albany to assume the governorship of the state, but he continued to play an active role in national affairs, swinging the northeastern states behind Andrew Jackson in his successful bid for the presidency. Jackson rewarded him with the post of secretary of state, so after only one year in the governor's mansion he headed back to Washington.

Politically adroit, able to grasp details quickly and to use them to best effect, Van Buren became the most powerful member of the cabinet and the one advisor whose judgment the President trusted most. In 1842, when Jackson made his winning race for reelection, Van Buren was his vice presidential running mate.

Now that he was well within striking distance of the highest office in the land, Vice President Van Buren set his sights firmly on capturing it. Throughout his vice presidential term he was exceedingly careful to keep all of his political fences well mended. The painstaking preparation paid off—in 1836 the Democratic Party nominated him as its presidential candidate. Master politician that he was, he knew exactly how he wanted to run his campaign.

Van Buren overlooked no segment of the voting public, fine-tuning his approach to each, but he was especially energetic in wooing the support of the largest single bloc of voters: those in rural and small-town America. To identify with them as closely as possible, he emphasized his origins on a Kinderhook farm, adopting the nickname of "Old Kinderhook" and campaigning vigorously under it. With his deft organizational touch, he stimulated establishment of scores of "Old Kinderhook" clubs to promote his candidacy. "Old Kinderhook" quickly became abbreviated to "O.K." and his booster clubs urged the public to "vote right, vote O.K." Van Buren made it into the White House and O.K. made it into the languages of the world as a synonym for "all right."

5

The Pleasure-Seekers

Ancient Greece had its Stoics who believed man should hold himself aloof from passion and joy, and its Spartans who believed man should be rigidly disciplined and austere (and from whom are derived stoic and spartan as name-words) but it also had its uninhibited, irresponsible revelers. Their feasts honoring Bacchus, god of wine, were such frenzied, drunken orgies that bacchanalia became a synonym for dissipation and debauchery. Things got so out-of-hand that in 186 B.C. the authorities finally banned bacchanalian carousing.

Rome followed in the footsteps of Athens. Romans paid tribute to Saturn, their god of the harvest, with such unrestrained feasting, drinking, and merrymaking that the world gained a second name-word for excessive carousing: saturnalia. Either saturnalia were not so abandoned as bacchanalia or Roman authorities were more lenient than

Greek because Rome adopted no law banning them.

In one way or another, man always seemed to take his amusements seriously, pursuing them with single-minded vigor that sometimes became self-indulgent excess. Frequently that pursuit was fueled by alcohol and sometimes the pursuer wound up in the ranks of the eponymous. It was true in Athens and Rome, and is still true. The very symbol of modern conviviality, the martini, is a name-word born in New York's old Waldorf Hotel when the bartender created both the cocktail and its name for a Señor Martinez, a pleasure-seeking Bolivian industrialist. Its first cousin, the gibson, emerged a short time later at the nearby Players Club when the bartender, out of olives, substituted an onion in the martini he made for Charles Dana Gibson, the famed artist. It was the second time Gibson became eponymous. The first was when his talented brush gave birth to the Gibson Girl, the beauty who became the cult of that generation the way Farrah Fawcett enthralled its descendants.

Eponyms seemed to flourish in the soil of the Waldorf. There was, for instance, Samuel Benedict, a notorious turn-of-the-century playboy. After a night of revelry he went to the Waldorf to pull himself together with a restorative breakfast. On the spur of the moment he conjured up an original dish he believed would do the trick: two poached eggs nestled on bacon resting on buttered toast and topped with Hollandaise sauce. The concoction restored him as he had thought it would. In addition, it was a tasty dish. Impressed, the Waldorf added it to its menu, substituting ham for the bacon and a muffin for the toast, and named it eggs Benedict after its playboy inventor.

Ben Wenberg, another New Yorker of the same era, did not fare quite as well as Samuel Benedict. A wealthy, fun-loving sea captain, when he was in port he sought his pleasures energetically to compensate for his long, boringly uneventful ocean voyages. Returning from one dull voyage, Captain Wenberg headed for his favorite restaurant, Delmonico's, carrying with him a pouch of hot cayenne pepper he had picked up abroad. Bent on making up for lost time, he paused lengthily at the bar before moving on to the kitchen where, aided by the chef, he cooked up an original dish utilizing his hot pepper. What he devised was a flavorsome marriage of lobster, cream, butter, eggs, and the cayenne. It turned out so successfully that Delmonico's named it lobster Wenberg for its creator and made it a regular offering of the restaurant.

The name of Wenberg's creation turned out to be less enduring that the dish itself. One evening, far from sober, the flamboyant sea captain arrived at the restaurant in a cantankerous mood. Loud and argumentative, he created a disturbance. Taking its revenge, Delmonico's continued serving the popular dish but reversed the "w" and the "n," so that lobster Wenberg became lobster Newberg. For good measure, it later altered the spelling to Newburg. Thus, Ben Wenberg's pugnaciousness got him alphabetized into second-class eponymic standing.

It would be inaccurate and unjust to leave the impression that the only revelers who gain admission to the ranks of the eponymous are those with a weakness for the bottle. It often helps, but it isn't a mandatory prerequisite. More than a thirst for strong drink, their common denominator is the persistence of their scramble after amusement.

As the pages that follow demonstrate, they foraged for their amusements in a variety of pastures and a variety of ways—from gaming table to drawing room to athletic arena. Some even found themselves eponymous not so much as a by-product of their own search for their pleasures as by their catering to others seeking theirs. Like Cèsar Ritz whose hotel guests basked so pleasurably in the lavish elegance he provided for them that ritzy became an international synonym for luxury and flair. Or like Richard Tattersall who opened a London horse market that became a favorite gathering place for gamblers and carousers. In a spirit of good-natured whimsy, the regulars at Tattersall's began wearing shirts of material designed like his horse blankets: a grid of thin vertical and horizontal lines on a solid background. The custom spread to more refined circles and tattersall became a durable name-word for a textile design that remains popular on both sides of the Atlantic.

George Bryan Brummell

As the eighteenth century was winding down, one would have had to eavesdrop long and hard to overhear British blue bloods mention the war their country had recently lost to its American colonies. It was not that England's upper classes were not chagrined that General Washington's ragtag army had beaten them, it was simply that they had something more important on their minds: fashion. Men, even more than women, were passionately fond of discussing fashion and of dressing stylishly. It was an amusement on which they lavished immoderate attention.

Preening like peacocks, Englishmen of that era made a fetish of fashion. From elaborately curled, heavily perfumed and powdered wigs to gleaming boot buckles, they were ornate, carefully orchestrated sartorial compositions—satins, silks, and brocades in rainbow hues, starched cravats, butter-soft leathers, sleek fur trimmings, intricate embroidery, fancy jewelry. The Englishman of rank did not simply clothe his body, he costumed it. More accurately, his "gentleman's gentleman"—his valet—bore the major burden of feathering the peacock who employed him.

Being a gentleman's gentleman was no simple task. In addition to the arduous chore of maintaining the vast wardrobe in impeccable condition, the valet had to dress his master, an exacting duty often requiring over half an hour just to tie the starched cravat so that it puffed and curled properly without the slightest suggestion of a wrinkle. But if the valet's responsibilities were demanding and his work day long, he was better paid than the rest of the household staff.

When George Bryan Brummell was born in 1778 it was assumed that he would follow family tradition by becoming a gentleman's gentleman. From his earliest years he was painstakingly trained by the Brummells to appreciate the dictates of men's fashions and to become proficient in the duties that were the valet's lot. Then, when he was sixteen, his father died and as sole heir he inherited the tidy sum accumulated by the thrifty Brummells. Now on his own with sufficient funds to permit freedom of choice, George decided he did not want to be a gentleman's gentleman. He wanted to be a gentleman, to make his name mean something. Ignoring Brummell tradition, he enrolled in Oxford University.

It did not take long at Oxford for it to become apparent that George was not meant to be a scholar. Leaving the university, he tried next to carve a career for himself in the army. The parade ground turned out to be no more promising than the campus had been, so he put away his saber and bid the military farewell. Taking stock of his situation, George Brummell realized that the only thing he really understood was fashion and the only thing he really enjoyed was dressing elegantly. Since that was his pleasure and his talent, he resolved to make the most of it, to make himself the most stylishly dressed man in England, the one to whom all others would yield on matters of high fashion.

Seeking out the finest tailors, bootmakers, hatters, wigmakers, and jewelers, he made his wardrobe his vocation. He had fabrics for his clothes woven to his own specifications in colors and designs bearing his original touches. Each garment was shaped to patterns he modified as inspiration struck him, so that it never duplicated a garment worn by anyone else. His cravats were larger than those of others, and starched so heavily he could not turn his head but had to pivot his body to look around. His boots were polished like mirrors on the soles as well as the uppers and he walked on tiptoe to avoid marring those shiny bottoms.

It required three hours each morning for Brummell to

dress, even though he had a servant to help him. When he was finally satisfied with his appearance he promenaded in public where he was likely to be seen by London's most important people. Then he returned home to change into a completely fresh outfit for an afternoon promenade. He dressed in yet a third complete change for evening wear.

Wherever Brummell appeared he created a stir, women sighing in admiration, men drooling in envy. All London gushed over the splendor and innovation of his clothes and over the lordly confidence with which he wore them. Invitations to garden parties, balls, teas, and dinners showered down on him. Men of wealth and of title solicited his advice on their wardrobes.

Brummell played his role to the hilt—lofty, supremely self-assured, issuing unequivocal pronouncements on matters of styling. His position as undisputed arbiter of fashion was firmly fixed when the Prince of Wales sought his advice on his clothes and the two became close friends. After the Prince became King George IV, he consulted Brummell as frequently on affairs of fashion as he consulted his ministers on affairs of state. Brummell now had a title of his own, "Beau" from the French for "beauty," an accolade bestowed on him by an adoring public.

There was only one cloud on Beau Brummell's horizon—he had spent his entire inheritance on clothes. To continue his lordly manner of living he began borrowing from his many wealthy friends, all of them pleased to use the power of their purses to cement relations with the man who was the dictator of fashion and the intimate of George

IV. For years Brummell managed to support his extravagances by borrowing, sometimes paying off an old debt by creating a new one.

Eventually, Brummell's army of creditors became restless. They commenced, politely enough at first, to press him for repayment. When this got no results they became more forceful. Brummell realized that time was running out. To escape drowning in his sea of debts he fled to France.

Settling in Caen, a city distant enough to be beyond easy reach of creditors yet close enough for his reputation as England's most stylish dresser to be well known, Beau Brummell tried to glue together the shattered pieces of his career. It seemed for a while that he would succeed. He became the center of a new circle of fashion-conscious admirers and was able to borrow from his new friends as he had from his old. However, the French are usually brief in their toleration of unpaid debts. Least tolerant of all are bankers. It was a banker who had him jailed for nonpayment of a sum due him.

Prison was a withering experience for Beau Brummell; it broke his health, stripped him of confidence and lordly pretensions. When he was finally released, he was a beaten man, penniless, friendless, dressed in rags. Living in squalor, scrounging in garbage cans for food, he was a sad sight—sick, emaciated, partially paralyzed. On March 30, 1840, he died in a pauper's hospital in Caen and was buried, unmourned, in an unmarked grave. He had done what he had set out to do as a young man in England—he had made his name mean something. But to bestow on posterity Beau Brummell as a name-word meaning a fashion-struck fop hardly seems a noble accomplishment.

Jules Léotard

The circus in modern form was in its infancy in 1859 when a twenty-one-year-old French acrobat, Jules Léotard, stepped into the spotlight in Paris' ornate, one-ring *Cirque Napoleon*. He stopped the show with a history-making performance and no circus would ever again be quite the same.

Until then, equestrian acts featuring trick riders had been the star performers. Acrobats and jugglers had played secondary, supporting roles. Léotard—lithe, muscular, already an accomplished acrobat when he was barely into his teens—had a streak of vanity in his makeup. His pride as a performing artist was offended by being billed second to the trick riders. After that night in the *Cirque Napoleon* he would never again suffer the indignity of second billing. What he did on that historic night was to introduce into the circus an exciting innovation he had conceived and perfected: the flying trapeze. The spectators had settled back into their seats for an evening of fun and entertainment— Léotard brought them leaping to their feet in amazement.

Executing acrobatics on a taut rope high above the arena floor was challenge enough for any professional aerialist. To perform them while hurtling through the air on a swinging trapeze was sensational. The cheers from the thrilled spectators were deafening. Rejoicing in the adulation of the fans, Léotard was not yet finished. He electrified his audience a second time when he executed the world's first aerial somersault.

No aerialist since then has captivated circus-goers in quite the same way as audacious, inventive Jules Léotard did. He also gave the females in his audiences an additional reason to adore him, as they did by the thousands. If he was daring in his performance, he was equally daring in his costume. He wore a single, thin garment of his own design. Clinging to his torso like a second skin, it revealed every curve and plane, every rippling muscle of his athletic body. Ever since, his costume has been known by the name-word he inspired: leotards.

Kid McCoy

There is a long tradition among young boxers of adopting the name of a ring star of the past—partly in the superstitious hope that some of his success will rub off on their gloves, partly in the reasonable belief that its familiar sound will lure fans to their matches. William Harrison Dempsey did it when he left the fields of rural Colorado to climb into the professional ring more than a half-century ago. Reaching back to 1884 to borrow the name of the then middleweight champion, he restyled himself Jack Dempsey, won the heavyweight crown in 1919, and created a record-book oddity that shows Jack Dempsey as both the middleweight and heavyweight champion with a span of thirty-five years between the two titles.

This penchant for recycling ring names is flattering to the old-timer, but in at least one case it turned out to be almost a knockout blow for one of them. It happened to Kid McCoy, who dominated the welterweight ranks from 1896 to 1900. Fast, hard-hitting, and ringwise, he was very popular and many young fighters of the day tried to model themselves on him. The trouble was that some of them were not content merely to copy his style of fighting; they also copied his name, even though he was still active in the ring. This created pugilistic confusion on a grand scale. With several Kid McCoys on the scene, fans often stayed away from matches featuring the original one under the mistaken impression that it involved a name-borrower. Even worse, when a copycat McCoy lost a fight, many of the confused fans pinned the loss on the original.

Trying to find a way out of the trap, the harried boxer began billing himself as Kid "The Real" McCoy to distinguish himself from all his imitators. The strategy worked. McCoy's new billing succeeded in setting him apart from the many name-borrowers, but it had come too late to do him much good. He was past his prime and soon faded from the sports scene. However, he turned out to be more durable in eponymy than in pugilism. Linguistically, the real McCoy is still going strong as a name-word for the genuine article.

John Montagu

When John Montagu was eleven, in 1729, his father died and he became fourth Earl of Sandwich, assuming the title vacated by his father's death. Had he been older, more mature in attitude as well as age when he succeeded to his earldom, things might have turned out differently. As it was, he tolerated formal schooling for only a few more years and then embarked on a long, leisurely tour of Europe during which he met all the right people and many of the wrong ones. He absorbed from them an appreciation of how politicians maneuver, a fondness for carousing, and a weakness for gambling. When he returned home in 1739 to take his seat in the House of Lords, he was an amusing conversationalist, a shrewd politician, and a compulsive gambler.

In 1741 the Earl of Sandwich married Judith, daughter of Viscount Fane. Poor Judith seldom saw her husband —though not so seldom that she did not regularly become pregnant—because he was so occupied with politics, partying, and cardplaying (and later with a female companion who bore him five children). He had little time left for the role of husband save on a part-time basis.

Making the most of his political and social connections, the Earl had himself named a lord commissioner of the navy and, simultaneously, an army colonel. Though there is no indication that he ever actually assumed the functions of a colonel, he was soon promoted to general. At the same time, he advanced to the post of First Lord of the Admiralty, the Royal Navy's highest office. Unlike his phantom duties as a general, as First Lord he was diligent in supervising the naval establishment. A powerful voice in military matters, he was also important in civil affairs, serving twice as secretary of state for the northern department and once as postmaster general.

Nobody disparaged the Earl's administrative ability, but his incorruptibility was another story. It was persistently rumored that he accepted bribes in awarding government contracts, exchanged public jobs for political favors, and permitted—and profited from—theft of government supplies from storage depots. Those making the charges gave him the derogatory nickname of Jemmy Twitcher, after a slippery character in *The Beggar's Opera.*

While political allies praised him and critics labeled him a Jemmy Twitcher, London's gambling clubs doted on the Earl of Sandwich, for he was one of their most consistent patrons. His favorite was the Beefsteak Club where in 1762 he performed the act that made him forever an international name-word. He had been at the card table for twenty-four hours without a halt, not even to eat. His hunger was great but his compulsion to continue play was even greater. Conceiving a way to satisfy one without infringing on the other, he called for a slice of beef and a slice of bread. Placing the meat on the bread, he was able to eat with one hand and play his cards with the other. His innovation was promptly dubbed a sandwich in his honor. (He did not actually invent the sandwich; it had been known even in Roman times but it was he who launched the neglected sandwich into universal popularity.) It is fortunate the name-word was not taken from his nickname—a bologna twitcher just would not do.

Sixteen years after that evening at the Beefsteak Club the

eponymous source of the sandwich inspired a second name-word. Because he had promoted British exploration vigorously, when Captain James Cook discovered a group of Pacific islands in 1778 he named them the Sandwich Islands. The second name-word derived from the Earl was less lasting than the first—in 1810 the Sandwich Islands became the Hawaiian Islands.

Edward Stanley

If medals were awarded for partying, Edward Stanley, twelfth Earl of Derby, would have been one of the most decorated men in history. He was one of England's most dedicated party-givers and party-goers. In fact, in 1772 he leased from his uncle a large building, once an alehouse, for the sole purpose of using it for his entertaining. (Uncle should have stayed around to enjoy the fun. Instead, he —General John Burgoyne—wound up commanding a British army during the American Revolution. Mauled by a force under General Horatio Gates at Saratoga, New York, in 1777, he was forced to surrender his army.)

Invitations to Stanley's romps were sought avidly because they were lavish, boisterous affairs, always offering a cockfight as an exciting diversion, since the Earl was enthusiastic about cockfighting. But perhaps his greatest zeal was reserved for horse racing. Paradise for him was to spend his days watching the thoroughbreds run and his nights entertaining friends.

It was this passion for horses that led him in 1780 to establish at Epsom Downs in Surrey a special race for three-year-old fillies. It quickly became the premier event of the British racing season. It continues to be England's most prestigious race and continues to be called the Derby in deference to its eponymous founder. As it turned out, however, there would be more name-words derived from the Earl than just the Epsom Downs classic.

The next name-word was a long time in coming and it developed in a roundabout way. In 1850 William Coke, tired of having his tall hat knocked from his head by low branches whenever he took his horse for a canter in the woods, resolved to do something about it. He went for help to James Lock and Company, then—and still—London's foremost hatters. Lock designed a totally new hat for Coke—low-crowned, melon-shaped, to be fabricated of felt strengthened with shellac to make it crush-resistant. Lock turned its design over to a manufacturer for production and the result was everything that had been hoped for it. Others, envying Coke his new hat, clamored for duplicates, calling it a bowler for the manufacturer, Thomas and William Bowler. Lock and Company, a rather starchy firm with a rigid sense of the fitness of things, insisted on calling it a coke for the man for whom they designed it; Lock's catalogue still lists it as a coke. Then, years after he was laid away in his final resting place, the Earl of Derby got into the act.

It happened this way: Americans visiting the track at Epsom Downs were smitten with the melon-shaped hat they saw so many Derby spectators wearing; when they returned home they brought it with them, calling it a derby for the

event where they discovered it. Practical as well as fashionable, the hat became a coast-to-coast favorite, giving the Earl
of Derby an eponymical beachhead in the New World.
(Americans were not the only foreigners smitten with the
hat. Visiting London in 1930, the King of Afghanistan was
fascinated by the bowler-coke-derby. He ordered dozens for
members of his court, but a problem arose when his cour-
tiers, practicing Moslems, touched their foreheads to the
ground during prayers. The brims touched first, flipping
the hats from their heads. To halt the flipping, they cut off
the brims of their new hats and wore only the crowns.)

The Earl of Derby's linguistic beachhead in America expanded when his name-word was adopted in 1875 for the
turf classic known as the Kentucky Derby. Later generations
broadened the meaning to include other contests from
soap-box to demolition derbies. So Edward Stanley—the
partying, cockfighting, horse-fancying, twelfth Earl of
Derby—left a large imprint on language.

6

The Female of the Species

Relatively few women have ever become eponymous, which may merely demonstrate that male chauvinism is sufficiently widespread to affect even language. However, the very first woman on earth—the first, that is, according to Greek mythology—did become an eponym. As legend has it, when the gods created Pandora they endowed her with near perfection and sent her down to man bearing a box they had warned her never to open. Pandora's single imperfection was a nagging curiosity. Succumbing to it, she opened the box, thereby releasing the evils with which the gods had filled it and which have ever since beset the world. Consequently, to uncover a source of troublesome problems is to open a Pandora's box.

Though eponymous females may be few in number, nobody can charge them with lacking either color or variety. Two well-established, female-inspired name-words offer proof of this contention. Oddly, both of them—maudlin and tawdry—came into being as a result of the completely opposite attitude with which the eponymous source of each regarded her virginity. One relinquished hers very young and very readily. The other clung to hers tenaciously, even after marriage.

The first member of this odd couple is the Biblical prostitute, Mary Magdalene, who encountered Christ, repented her transgressions, and was forgiven by Him. A deeply sentimental woman, softhearted and easily moved to tears, she became a favorite subject of painters of religious scenes. The artists invariably captured her on their canvases in a sorrowful pose, shedding tears for her Redeemer and His sacrifice, tears for her past. Forever doleful, forever weeping, her name gradually came to be a synonym for excessive sentimentality. But the British, who pronounce Worcester as Wooster and Cholmondeley as Chumlee, could be expected to do to Magdalene what those with less innovative tongues would not attempt—they pronounced it as Maudlin and when it became a name-word its spelling followed its sound. (One of the institutions at Great Britain's noted Cambridge University is Magdalene College. Rival Oxford University has its Magdalen College. Both institutions, one with a final "e" and one without, are pronounced "Maudlin.")

Seven centuries after Mary Magdalene, Ethelreda was born in England. She had little in common with the sentimental, repentant prostitute. She was highborn, daughter of an Anglo-Saxon king, and she had nothing to repent, having from the start adhered unfailingly to principles of unimpeachable morality. Where Mary Magdalene came to Christianity after she was an adult, Princess Ethelreda was consumed by religious fervor while still a child.

As Ethelreda grew into young womanhood her religious zeal grew even stronger. She knew she would have to yield her hand in marriage to whichever royal suitor her father selected for her, but she was determined to yield no more than her hand, to keep her body an undefiled temple for the soul within it she had dedicated to God. So she married the chosen suitor and when he sickened and died three years later he had not progressed beyond his wife's hand.

Once again a royal marriage was arranged and once again Ethelreda fended off her husband, despite his impassioned pleading. After twelve years during which he failed to wear down his wife's resistance, he realized his cause was hopeless. Frustrated, he agreed to allow his virginal wife to leave him to take up the life of a nun.

Happily trading the trappings of royalty for the veil of a nun, Princess Ethelreda, now known as Audrey, went to the east of England where she founded a monastery. Her piety and dedication attracted many others to her side. With Audrey as abbess, the monastery flourished into an important religious center, unusual in that it included monks as well as nuns. Called Saint Audrey by her flock, when she died the revered abbess was buried at the monastery she had nurtured. Her burial place became a shrine visited by throngs of the faithful, especially during religious holidays. Where there are throngs there are also the inevitable hawkers of souvenirs. The mementoes they peddled were cheap, gaudy trinkets that they dubbed "Saint Audreys." Before long their huckstering chant of "Saint Audrey" had become shortened and corrupted into "tawdry." Thus, there is the paradox of the virgin princess, so pious and above reproach, who would forever be memorialized by a name-word that stands for cheap, vulgar tastelessness.

From Mary Magdalene and Ethelreda to Phoebe Anne Oakley Mozee is a journey of hundreds of years and thousands of miles—to rural Darke County, Ohio, where she was born in 1860. Every youth in the area—thinly populated, wooded, rich in game—learned early how to use a hunting rifle with the same ease and skill with which he learned to farm. There was a tomboy streak in Annie and she, too, took to the woods with a rifle at an early age. A natural hunter with quick reflexes and remarkable eye-hand coordination, she developed surprising proficiency with her rifle. Her father died while she was still a child and it was her hunting rifle that put meat on the family table. Branching out, Annie began practicing with pistols and became as effective with them as with long guns.

At the urging of friends, when Annie was fifteen she entered a shooting match in nearby Cincinnati pitting Frank E. Butler, a vaudeville marksman, against all comers. Butler assumed Annie was joking when she entered the match, but with her first shots he realized his error. She won the contest. What began as a lark ended on a serious note—she and Butler fell in love, married, and started touring the vaudeville circuit as a trick-shooting team.

In 1885 the couple joined Buffalo Bill Cody's Wild West Show, but it was Annie who was now clearly the star of the act. Billed as "Miss Annie Oakley, the Peerless Lady Wing

Shot," she thrilled audiences with her dazzling marksman-
ship. At 30 yards she split a playing card held edgewise, and
shot a cigarette from her husband's lips. To climax the act,
her husband tossed a card into the air and she riddled it
with bullet holes before it hit the ground. Annie continued
her remarkable shooting exhibitions until 1902. By that
time her feat of riddling a card with holes had made Annie
Oakley the popular term for complimentary tickets that
ushers cancelled by punching holes in them. (Later, the
story of Phoebe Anne Oakley Mozee would serve as the
theme for the long-running Broadway musical, *Annie Get
Your Gun.*)

Alexandrina Victoria and Annie Oakley were cut from
different molds. Where Annie was outgoing, hearty and
fun-loving, she was straitlaced, reserved, prim, and formal.
Where Annie was raised in humble surroundings, she was
raised amid great wealth and ceremony. Where Annie's
education was haphazard and her manners bluff and direct,
Alexandrina Victoria's were impeccable. Yet, despite all of
that there were still some similarities. Both embarked on
notable careers while still in their teens and both ultimately
became eponymous.

When she was eighteen in 1837, Alexandrina Victoria
succeeded to the British throne. As Queen Victoria, she
reigned for a record sixty-four years. She also established a
record as the inspiration for more, and more varied,
name-words than any other female before or since. Her
name (or such forms of it as Victorian and Victorine) was
adopted for social attitudes that were so prim as to be
prudish, for styles of architecture and of furniture that

were noted for their ostentation and—frequently—for their poor craftsmanship, for a four-wheeled carriage and an open touring car, for a fur scarf, a water lily, a military medal, and for the whole period of history during which she ruled Great Britain. (Her royal consort, Prince Albert, also became eponymous but he was left far, far behind by Victoria; his name was adopted only for a long, double-breasted frock coat.)

Prostitution, religion, vaudeville, statecraft—eponymous women set their feet on strikingly different paths on their journeys toward becoming a part of language. Here are more of the varied paths they followed.

Amelia Jenks Bloomer

Shock waves that rocked the nation in 1851 were generated from an unlikely spot—Seneca Falls in the peaceful lake region of western New York. The detonator that set off those shock waves was even less likely—Amelia Jenks Bloomer, the small town's respected assistant postmaster.

It all began because Amelia Bloomer was staunchly opposed to alcoholic beverages. She steadfastly condemned anything immoral or demeaning, but in her view the chief social ill was alcohol. She spoke out against it and wrote articles for local newspapers urging the benefits of abstinence. But she craved a wider platform for her views and to gain it she founded *The Lily*, the first women's magazine to appear in America. Nominally, the magazine was the official publication of the Seneca Falls Ladies' Temperance Society, but in actual fact it was all Amelia's, the product of her energy and effort.

The Lily was a lively magazine, stimulating its readers and pricking their consciences. Circulation grew over an ever-expanding region and as it did, the editor's influence grew with it. Having gained a position of prominence among women, she was sought out increasingly by feminist leaders hoping to have her join a coordinated effort to eliminate inequities imposed on women by male-dominated society. Amelia Bloomer listened sympathetically but was not wholly convinced. It wasn't that she was not a social activist at heart; it was that she chose her causes carefully. Happily married, never having been knowingly subjected to gross injustice because of her sex, she considered feminist issues less urgent than the alcohol problem. And then she met Elizabeth Smith Miller.

Daughter of a wealthy, liberal philanthropist, Elizabeth Miller was an independent thinker, a rebel against prevailing male beliefs pigeonholing women into second-class status politically, economically, and other ways. To dramatize her rejection of male, self-proclaimed superiority, she wore in public a unique, male-baiting costume of her own design. Consisting of long, loose-fitting pantaloons gathered at the ankles and worn beneath a dress so short that it was little longer than a blouse, it was exceedingly "daring" for the times. (A centuries-old name-word, pantaloons comes from Pantaleone, the elderly buffoon in an early Venetian comedy who wore trousers that bagged and sagged from waist to knee and then clung skin-tight down to his ankles.)

CARL A. RUDISILL LIBRARY
LENOIR RHYNE COLLEGE

Amelia Bloomer outfitted herself in a replica of the Miller costume, but not for the same reason as its designer. She adopted it simply because she considered that it made good sense, since it liberated the body from the restrictions of the clumsy, impractical hoopskirt, enabling women to move about as comfortably as men.

Seneca Falls was aghast when she appeared on its streets in her pantaloons and mini-skirt. Not content merely to wear the costume, she took it up as a cause. Using the pages of *The Lily* as her forum, she called on her readers to switch from hoopskirts to pantaloons. From coast to coast, great numbers heeded her appeal. Immediately, the bloomers —as everyone began terming them for their ardent booster—became a national issue.

Church leaders, condemning bloomers as immoral and scandalous, preached against them from their pulpits. Public figures, choosing their side according to their conservative or liberal attitude, debated the matter. Newspapers trumpeted the issue in news columns, editorials, and cartoons. Households across the land bristled with argument between wives favoring bloomers and husbands hostile to them. Bloomers even crossed the ocean to England where a number of women donned them, causing repercussions similar to those in America.

The opponents of bloomers did not pull their punches. It required determination and a thick skin to persist in wearing the garment in public in the face of the ridicule and the smirks that were so common. Gradually, fewer and fewer bloomers were seen on the street and, after a few years of seeing her supporters melt away, even Amelia Bloomer

abandoned the controversial costume. But though she relinquished it, it did not relinquish her—it made her a
name-word reminder of one of the encounters in the long-
running conflict between the sexes.

Jeanne Antoinette Poisson

Appropriately, François Poisson, a Paris food merchant
whose name—Poisson—translates from French into English
as Fish, handled fish among other foodstuffs. Inappro-
priately, he had a weakness for crooked schemes. Caught
embezzling funds, he fled to Germany, leaving his wife behind to cope as best she could.

Coping was something Madame Poisson did well. She
found a wealthy, well-connected tax collector to console her
and in 1721, more than a year after her husband had fled,
gave birth to Jeanne Antoinette Poisson. Acknowledging his
paternity, the tax collector agreed to finance the girl's education.

If Monsieur Poisson was a Fish, Madame was a shark. She
spared no expense, since her lover would foot the bill, in
raising Jeanne Antoinette in a way to enable her to snare a
rich husband. She had a lot to work with—her daughter was
a pretty, graceful child with a quick, precocious mind. After
attending a convent school she was turned over to excellent
tutors for coaching in philosophy, the arts, literature, and
music. By the time she reached mid-teens she was arrest-
ingly beautiful—poised, seductive, able to converse sensibly,
wittily, charmingly.

Judging the time ripe for her daughter to marry, Madame Poisson chose Charles le Normant d'Étioles to be the groom, selecting him because he was wealthy, moved in the best circles, and could be maneuvered into her net through the well-placed connections of her lover. D'Étioles never stood a chance.

The marriage went well for a time—the groom delighted with the way his lovely wife captivated the important personages to whom he introduced her, the bride relishing her entrance into Paris society. But Madame Poisson considered d'Étioles only a stepping-stone. Audaciously, she set her sights on King Louis XV himself, despite the fact that he, as well as her daughter, was already married.

Studying Louis like a general planning an offensive, Madame Poisson plotted her moves adroitly, dispatching Jeanne Antoinette to the opera when Louis would be there, to balls where he was to appear, to ride in the woods where he was scheduled to hunt. Inevitably, Louis took note of the young beauty crossing his path so frequently. Leaving little to chance, the scheming mother bribed a court attendant to praise her daughter's qualities to Louis.

The campaign bore fruit—the King invited Jeanne Antoinette to an intimate dinner and the intimacy turned out to be ultimate, ending in the royal bedchamber. A few weeks later Louis invited Jeanne Antoinette to move into his palace at Versailles. She accepted. Her disconsolate husband, powerless to thwart the defection from his bed to the King's, was soothed somewhat when Louis granted him a lucrative government post.

French nobility, long accustomed to mistresses, took

Jeanne Antoinette in stride but muttered about her unbe-
coming background. She strove to win them over and at the
same time to strengthen her position in the affections of the
King. She was successful on both fronts. Even the Queen
became reconciled, because this mistress was at least cultured and properly respectful. Before the year was out
Louis draped a veil of concealment over Jeanne
Antoinette's unsavory past by creating her the Marquise de
Pompadour.

The new Marquise stretched her titled wings and soared.
Drawing on royal funds, she adorned herself with
magnificent gowns and gems. But these extravagances
faded into insignificance against her acquisition of several
chateaux that she furnished in a manner remarkable for
good taste as well as monumental cost. At this point,
Madame Poisson—an awkward reminder of the past-
—eliminated that awkwardness by dying. Having seen her
scheme culminate in dizzying success, she died happy.

With access to royal funds and genuine appreciation of
the arts, the Marquise de Pompadour sponsored numerous
promising painters, sculptors, and dramatists, and such
emerging philosophers as Rousseau and Voltaire. Convinced that France could produce porcelain to rival that of
China and Dresden, she organized the works at Sèvres that
created some of the most exquisite porcelain the world has
seen.

Europe saluted her cultural achievements with an explo-
sion of objects named for her—Pompadour sofas and
chairs, fans and vases, mirrors and gowns, and—from the
Sèvres works—a magnificent Pompadour porcelain. But the

most enduring name-word she inspired is the pompadour, describing the style she originated of dressing the hair in a high upsweep from the forehead.

Rich, cultured, and eponymous, the Marquise de Pompadour was now also a potent figure. Wielding great influence over Louis' decisions on affairs of state, the illegitimate adulteress had become the power behind the throne. Never was this more apparent than when she persuaded Louis to reverse foreign policy by seeking an alliance with France's traditional enemy, Austria. She herself negotiated the treaty of alliance. It cost France dearly, helping to bring about the devastating Seven Years' War and losing it most of its overseas possessions. (However, it aided the birth of the United States because France, so humiliated in the war, tried to regain some of its prestige by helping the rebelling Americans.)

In the aftermath of the Seven Years' War, Frenchmen looked for a scapegoat, finding it in the woman who negotiated the treaty leading to that conflict. Paris mobs reviled the Marquise de Pompadour as "that prostitute who governs the kingdom and is bringing it to ruin." But the war had been no kinder to her than to them. Worn and wearied by strain, she lay ill at Versailles. She died there on April 15, 1764, at the age of forty-two. In her will she deeded Louis her Paris mansion; today that mansion of the "prostitute who governed the kingdom"—the Elysée Palace—is the official residence of the President of France.

It is ironic that the remarkable woman who caused French culture to flourish, exerted a profound influence on the affairs of France, and left an imprint on international history, should be remembered for a little more than that she was mistress of a king and eponymous innovator of a hair style.

Helen Porter Mitchell

Almost from the moment of her birth in Melbourne, Australia, in 1861, two things became the twin trademarks that would distinguish Helen Porter Mitchell throughout her life. The first was the nickname "Nellie" bestowed on her by her family and friends alike. The second was a deep, passionate love for singing. Wherever Nellie was, there was song. Even as a very young child, her voice—sweet and bell-like—was a joy to hear. As she grew older her life became more and more centered around her music. There was within her a compulsion, a hunger to sing.

Nellie and song had become so steadfastly intertwined that it was taken for granted by all who knew her that she would pursue a serious career in music. But it was clear to everyone that the Melbourne of that era, still largely a cultural wasteland, was hardly the place to obtain the kind of sensitive, highly skilled professional training she required. So her family sent her to Paris to study under Mathilde Marchessi, a noted voice teacher.

Madame Marchessi was a demanding perfectionist, Nellie a devoted and tireless student. The two suited each other admirably, each a challenge to the best that was in the other. Month by month there was discernible improvement in Nellie's performance, an emerging subtlety of interpretation and mastery of technique that had only been hinted at previously.

Neither the teacher nor the pupil was deluded by the progress being made. Each realized that it was only a beginning, that the distance they had come was only a small step along the road yet to be traveled. The months stretched into years that were demanding and emotion-draining to each. But they were also rewarding years, for it was clear that the girl from Melbourne was making the difficult transition from good singer to great singer.

On a cold and rainy November evening in 1887, Nellie made her professional debut in the Brussels Opera House. Under the stage name of Nellie Melba, which she coined in tribute to her native Melbourne, she sang the role of Gilda in *Rigoletto*. It was a triumphant debut. The audience rose to its feet, cheering wildly. In their newspaper reviews the next morning, the critics could not find superlatives enough to describe her performance. The opera world proclaimed Nellie as the soprano of the century.

All Brussels vied for the honor of entertaining the new star of the opera stage. The chef of the Cafe Bruges, the city's leading restaurant, rose to the occasion when a reception for Nellie was held in his establishment. He invented a new and sumptuous dessert for the gala dinner—a poached peach on an ice cream base and bathed in raspberry sauce—and named it peach Melba.

Nellie Melba's remarkable career brought her glory on the world's leading operatic stages—including the Metropolitan in New York where she sang repeatedly from 1893 to 1910—and as she progressed from triumph to triumph other chefs followed the lead of the Cafe Bruges, so that she became the eponymous inspiration for such offerings as pears Melba, Melba sauce, and Melba toast. Very soon after she retired, another soprano—the Italian Luisa Tetrazzini—dazzled opera lovers and she, too, became eponymous when a New York chef invented a calorie-laden dish and named it chicken Tetrazzini. Some critics were convinced that she sang as superbly as Nellie Melba had. But if one could debate their relative merit as singers, there was no doubt of their relative standing as eponyms. Luisa Tetrazzini, with only one name-word to her credit, was obviously Nellie Melba's eponymic inferior.

7

Born on the End of a Pen

The story would be incomplete without dipping, however briefly, into the rich brew of eponymous figures who were conceived in an author's imagination and were born on the end of his pen. Fictional characters though they may be, through the name-words they have inspired many of them have assumed a vitality and a longevity that put them in the same league as flesh-and-blood eponyms. Who can fail to find animation and substance in Shakespeare's relentless moneylender who made shylock a disparaging name-word, or in Cervantes' foolishly romantic idealist who made quixotic a gently mocking term, or in Dickens' heartless miser who made scrooge an insult, or in Spenser's blustering boaster, Braggadocio, who made brag, braggart, and braggadocio tart name-words? To shun eponyms like these merely because there is ink in their veins is to disregard much of the appeal of eponymy and, sometimes, to miss out on some of its surprises.

One fictional eponym who would seem to possess few surprises is Shakespeare's well-known lover, Romeo, who pursued Juliet with such passion that his name has become a description for ardent lovers everywhere. Yet, even on such familiar ground the unexpected manages to rear its head. Contrary to widely held belief, Shakespeare was not actually Romeo's literary father. At best, he was no more than a kind of great-uncle. The fact is that Shakespeare copied his Romeo from the impassioned suitor in *Romeus and Juliet,* a fourteenth-century poem. But Romeus himself was also a literary clone, having been copied from the lover in earlier works. In truth, the lovelorn hero panted his way through so many writings, including no less than eighteen different operas, that the popular name-word emerging from these amatory episodes has a whole community of lovers as its eponymous source.

It was not passionate affection, it was disaffection that influenced George Ruggle, one of Shakespeare's fellow playwrights. Ruggle was a man of strong opinions and he had no hesitancy in expressing them. One of his deepest convictions was that lawyers were an obnoxious lot —egotistical, arrogant, and, more than anything else, dim-witted. To provide a forum for voicing his disaffection for lawyers he wrote a play in 1615 in which the leading character was a bumbling lawyer. To make sure that nobody would miss his point, Ruggle gave his play and its main character the same name—*Ignoramus*—Latin for "We don't know." The mental shortfall displayed by the stage lawyer made so lasting an impression on audiences that they

adopted ignoramus as a name-word for any poorly informed person, member of the bar or not.

Many things were said about Francois Rabelais but never
that he was poorly informed. Religiously oriented, as a
young man he received a very thorough, basic education as
a novice in a Franciscan monastery in his native France. He
broadened his scholarly interests after he became a monk,
delving deeply into the classics, the sciences, philosophy,
and languages. Then he arranged to transfer to the Benedictine order to continue expanding his academic horizons in the highly regarded Benedictine institutions. Still
hungry for knowledge, he obtained permission from his ec-
clesiastical superiors to study medicine, earning his medical
degree from the University of Montpelier in 1532.

From Montpelier, Rabelais went to Lyons where he established a medical practice and also undertook to edit Latin
works for various publishing houses. At the same time, he
began writing what all the world would one day come to
hail as a masterpiece. A monumental project that eventually
ran to five volumes, it was a brilliant blend of humor and of
seriousness, of burlesque and of philosophical insights.
When he was writing seriously, Rabelais displayed scholarship and keen perception. However, when he was writing in
a comic vein he demonstrated an earthy, ribald sense of
humor that was surprising in one so closely linked to the
church.

The first of his five volumes constituted an attack on the
ostentatious extravagances of French royalty, but Rabelais
was not about to risk his neck by a foolhardy direct con-

demnation of the throne and those around it. Instead, he wrote about a giant, loud-mouthed, imaginary king; everyone understood that this was pretense, that behind the subterfuge of his imaginary king he was really referring to the French royalty of that period.

The giant, he wrote, was so enormous at birth and so greedy that it took 17,913 cows to provide him with milk. When he reached his full growth it required 1,100 hides to make a pair of his shoes and the horse he rode was as large as six elephants. Grasping, always greedy for more, his appetite was so huge that it defied comparison. Rabelais named his fictitious king Gargantua and ever since then anything of enormous dimensions has been called gargantuan. The author, like his imaginary king, also became eponymous when the ribald humor of his books led to adoption of Rabelasian as a name-word for bawdy.

Where Rabelais was a multitalented phenomenon making his mark as monk, physician, editor, and author, Mrs. Susanna Centlivre concentrated her efforts on writing alone. She reached the high point of her literary career in 1718 when she turned out *A Bold Stroke for a Wife,* an amusing, popular play whose chief character was an eminently respectable Quaker. The plot of the play revolved around the Quaker's troubles with an unscrupulous and immoral impostor whose impersonation of him created havoc in his life. From the staid and harassed hero—Simon Pure —comes simon-pure as a name-word for the genuine, uncorrupted article.

Not very long after simon-pure settled into its niche as a part of the language, a new dramatist was capturing attention in England. Richard Brinsley Sheridan, like Rabelais before him, was a man of many talents (and a few flaws, notably a weakness for the bottle and a disinclination to pay his bills on time). He wrote plays that sparkled with wit, poetry that was sensitive, and a comic opera for which his father-in-law composed the music. He became the owner and, for a time, the stage director of London's famous Drury Lane Theater. And he was quite active in political life, at one point serving as undersecretary of foreign affairs and at another as a member of Parliament where he dazzled that body with his brilliant oratory and dramatic gestures.

Sheridan's two most notable comedies were *The Rivals* and *The School for Scandal.* Audiences roared at the character in *The Rivals,* Mrs. Malaprop, who had a habit of confusing her words, saying one thing when she really meant to say something else that sounded similar. Tripping over her amusing tongue, she came out with such mix-ups as "contagious" countries for "contiguous" countries, "illiterate" for "obliterate," and "dissolve" for "resolve." It was the kind of thing Archie Bunker amuses modern TV viewers with when he says "physical" year instead of "fiscal" year or "incinerated" in place of "insinuated." Because of the popularity of Mrs. Malaprop and her errant tongue, she became enshrined in the ranks of the eponymous so that Archie and every other tongue-twister who have followed her have been uttering malapropisms.

Like Sheridan who preceded him by a half-century as a darling of British theater-goers, James Kenney had a talent for writing plays that were buoyant with good humor and spirited dialogue. He knew he had an instant hit on his hands when he opened his farce, *Raising the Wind,* on the London stage. What made Kenney's comedy hum along so merrily was its major character, a lovable, fast-talking swindler and con man, Jeremy Diddler. Almost overnight the language was refreshed with a perky, new name-word. People were no longer hoodwinked; they were diddled.

Taking his place in the long procession of the eponymous—the paragons of virtue and the rascals, the wise and the foolish, the vain and the humble, the real and the fictitious—Jeremy Diddler became a part of the lively band parading through language to invigorate it with their name-words. It is a parade with no end, for always around the next bend in the road is another who will swell the ranks of the marchers. It is heartening, this parade without end, for it assures the continued enrichment of human communication with the vitality of the name-word contributions of the eponymous. What Carl Sandburg once said of slang is even more true of name-words—they are language that takes off its coat, spits on its hands, and goes to work.

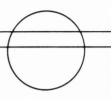

Index

THE AUTHOR

VERNON PIZER is the author of numerous books and of several hundred articles in leading magazines in the United States, Europe, and the Far East. His work has been collected in anthologies, has been reprinted in many languages, and has been adopted as teaching aids by the U.S. Air Force Academy, Loyola University of Chicago, and many secondary schools.

The breadth of his interests is suggested by the variety of the subjects he has covered—foreign and military affairs, the sciences, social problems, sports, and travel—but the thread through all of his work is his emphasis on the people involved in the things he describes. His books include *Ink, Ark., and All That: How American Places Got Their Names* and *Glorious Triumphs: Athletes Who Conquered Adversity*.

After having lived in Washington, Paris, Vienna, and Turkey, Mr. Pizer and his wife, Marguerite, now make their home in Georgia.

TAKE
MY WORD
FOR IT

Vernon Pizer

When Cèsar Ritz created his luxurious hotels in Paris, New York, and elsewhere, he pampered his guests with such elegance and so many sumptuous comforts that the world adopted a new word —ritzy—as a synonym for lavish luxury. Thus, Cèsar Ritz became an eponym: the source of a word that is derived from a person's name. In becoming eponymous, he joined a remarkably diverse group— presidents and prizefighters, opera stars and gamblers. *Take My World for It* provides a grandstand seat from which to enjoy this fascinating parade.

But *Take My Word for It* doesn't merely parade the eponyms past the reader. It digs selectively into the little-known stories behind the individuals whose name-words give zest and meaning to language—from Frisbee to shrapnel, from dunce to silhouette, from boycott to diddle. Told engagingly and wittily, the accounts of the eponyms and the name-words they inspired are surprising, stimulating, often humorous, sometimes inspiring, but never dull. Take our word for it.